Representative American Speeches 2002–2003

Editors

Calvin M. Logue, Ph.D.

and

Lynn M. Messina, Ph.D.

The Reference Shelf
Volume 75 • Number 6

The H.W. Wilson Company
2003

The Reference Shelf

The books in this series contain reprints of articles, excerpts from books, addresses on current issues, and studies of social trends in the United States and other countries. There are six separately bound numbers in each volume, all of which are usually published in the same calendar year. Numbers one through five are each devoted to a single subject, providing background information and discussion from various points of view and concluding with a subject index and comprehensive bibliography that lists books, pamphlets, and abstracts of additional articles on the subject. The final number of each volume is a collection of recent speeches, and it contains a cumulative speaker index. Books in the series may be purchased individually or on subscription.

Library of Congress has cataloged this serial title as follows:

Representative American speeches. 1937 / 38–
    New York, H. W. Wilson Co.
       v. 21 cm.—The Reference Shelf
Annual
Indexes:
    Author index: 1937/38–1959/60, with 1959/60;
    1960/61–1969/70, with 1969/70; 1970/71–1979/80,
    with 1979/80; 1980/81–1989/90, 1990.
Editors: 1937/38–1958/59, A. C. Baird.—1959/60–1969/70, L. Thonssen.—1970/71–1979/80, W. W. Braden.—1980/81–1994/95, O. Peterson.—1995/96–1998/99 , C. M. Logue and J. DeHart.—1999/2000– , C. M. Logue and L. M. Messina.
    ISSN 0197-6923 Representative American speeches.
      1. Speeches, addresses, etc., American. 2. Speeches, addresses, etc.
      I. Baird, Albert Craig, 1883–1979 ed. II. Thonssen, Lester, 1904–
      III. Braden, Waldo Warder, 1911–1991 ed.
      IV. Peterson, Owen, 1924– ed. V. Logue, Calvin McLeod, 1935– , Messina, Lynn M.,
      and DeHart, Jean, eds. VI. Series.
PS668.B3   815.5082   38-27962
                                                        MARC-S
Library of Congress [8503r85] rev4

Cover: President George W. Bush speaking in Grand Rapids, Michigan, January 29, 2003. (AP Photo/Rick Bowmer)

Visit H. W. Wilson's Web site: www.hwwilson.com

Printed in the United States of America

Contents

Preface

By the end of the day on September 11, 2001, Americans realized that their nation and the world would never be the same, and public dialogue would bear that out. In 2002 and 2003 the event continued to shape individual behavior and public policy, and nowhere was this more evident than in the actions and speeches of the Bush administration. This book therefore contains a number of speeches by government leaders, such as President Bush, Colin Powell, and Tom Ridge. However, while Americans continued to be preoccupied with the ongoing War on Terror, many other issues also engaged the public attention, some of which are covered in the later chapters of this book.

The first chapter looks at the development of the Bush administration's foreign policy in response to the terrorist attacks of 2001. In the 2002 State of the Union address, President George W. Bush had suggested a connection between terrorism and the nation of Iraq, and as the year went on, his accusations and those of his administration grew louder. By September 2002 the president was speaking directly to the United Nations about a possible preemptive military strike against the regime of Iraqi president Saddam Hussein, which he claimed possessed weapons of mass destruction that made Iraq a threat, not just to the Middle East, but to the entire world. From that point on, no other issue dominated American discourse more than the impending war with Iraq. The speeches here present the administration's position on the war and foreign policy, as well as the voices of opposition to the president's stated objectives.

One of President Bush's aims in going to war with Iraq was to eliminate a threat to America's national security and to safeguard the country from future terrorist attacks. For the same reasons, he proposed the creation of a cabinet-level Department of Homeland Security (DHS), which would place several agencies, such as FEMA, the INS, and others, under one authority while coordinating the intelligence-gathering efforts of the FBI, NSA, and CIA. The drastic restructuring and consolidation of so many federal agencies made the creation of the department controversial, but in 2002, Congress approved the elevation of the department's head to a cabinet-level position, making Governor Tom Ridge of Pennsylvania the first secretary of the DHS. Chapter II looks at the activities and effectiveness of the new department in safeguarding America's transportation, ports, and water supply and considers areas that many believe need special attention, including the monitoring of foreign students and funding for first-responders.

The Bush administration's responses to September 11, including the wars in Afghanistan and Iraq and the creation of the Department of Homeland Security, have prompted much debate among ordinary Americans, all of it protected by the First Amendment to the U.S. Constitution. Nevertheless, many

Americans have felt their freedom of speech and other civil liberties under attack over the last two years, and they worry about such measures as the U.S.A. PATRIOT Act proposed by the president in the wake of the terrorist attacks. The speeches in Chapter III examine Americans' right to free expression on college campuses, in the media, and elsewhere, the degree to which it is currently threatened, and how much it should be limited—if at all—in the interests of national security.

While several of the issues presented in this volume are directly related to America's response to the terrorist attacks two years ago, others reflect additional concerns that speak to the very basic human desire to nurture the body and soul in an ever-changing world. One such issue that continued to make headlines across the nation during 2002 and 2003 was the welfare of children, especially those in the foster care system. State-funded foster care agencies are often understaffed and overburdened, allowing child abuse or neglect to go undetected until tragedy strikes, as it did in Newark, New Jersey, with the death of seven-year-old Faheem Williams in January 2003. Adoption may be the ultimate goal for these children, but even that process could be fraught with red tape and other difficulties, including emotional adjustments, that may discourage prospective parents. The speakers in Chapter IV discuss foster care and adoption while also looking at the effectiveness of other systems designed to care for children, such as child welfare, juvenile justice, mental health, and special education; the importance of giving American children a more international education; how the U.S. government might make children more of a priority in its public policy; and the effect of violent video games on children.

The final chapter in this book includes speeches reflecting on the adventurous nature of the human spirit, a boldness that endures even in the face of seemingly insurmountable challenges and tragic failures. This chapter contains baccalaureate addresses encouraging young graduates to face the often frightening new times in which we live by imposing their own vision on the world, despite the resistance of others to their innovations and creativity. The beginning of the 100th-anniversary year commemoration of the Wright brothers' historic first flight of December 17, 1903, is also celebrated here, along with the lives of the ill-fated crew of the Space Shuttle *Columbia*, which blew apart upon reentry into Earth's atmosphere on February 1, 2003, killing all seven astronauts aboard. The irreplaceable individuals who perished that day—along with their forefathers in flight, the Wright brothers—in many ways embodied the courage needed by Americans and all peoples to challenge preconceptions and explore possibilities beyond those conceived by ordinary men and women.

We would like to thank all of the speakers who generously gave us permission to reprint their speeches here. We would also like to thank Jennifer Peloso, Gray Young, Norris Smith, and Rich Stein for their assistance in producing this book.

December 2003

I. War and Foreign Policy

Testimony Before the House Committee on International Relations[1]

Colin L. Powell

U.S. secretary of state, 2001– ; born New York City, April 5, 1937, and raised in South Bronx; graduated Morris High School, New York City, 1954; B.S. in geology, City College of New York, 1958; M.B.A., George Washington University, 1971; U.S. army, 1958–93, including two tours in Vietnam (1962–63 and 1968–69); assistant to the president for national security affairs, 1987–89; promoted to rank of four-star general, 1989; chairman, Joint Chiefs of Staff, 1989-93, overseeing Operation Desert Storm in the 1991 Persian Gulf War; chairman, America's Promise—The Alliance for Youth, 1993–2001; author, My American Journey, *1995; two Presidential Medals of Freedom; President's Citizens Medal; Congressional Gold Medal; Secretary of State Distinguished Service Medal; Secretary of Energy Distinguished Service Medal; honorary degrees from several universities and colleges, including Yeshiva University; Purple Heart, Bronze Star, and Legion of Merit Award.*

Editors' introduction: After thousands of people were killed by terrorist assaults on New York City, Washington, D.C., and Shanksville, Pennsylvania, on September 11, 2001, in an address on September 20, 2001, President Bush assured the U.S. Congress and the American people that "our war" would "not end . . . until every terrorist group of global reach has been found, stopped and defeated." In a speech on September 12, 2002, to the United Nations, the president attempted to justify intervention in Iraq, which he insisted posed a danger to the U.S. and the world. One week later, in testimony before the U.S. House Committee on International Relations, Secretary of State Powell defended the administration's stance against Iraq. He insisted, "We can have debates, discussions and disagreements about the size and nature of the Iraqi stockpile of weapons of mass destruction, and we can discuss whether they are or are not violating the range constraints on the missiles that they have. But no one can doubt the record of Iraqi violations of United Nations Security Council resolutions."

---

1. Delivered September 19, 2002, Washington, D.C.

Colin L. Powell's speech: [Mr. Chairman, members of] the committee, I welcome this opportunity to present the administration's position with respect to our situation regarding Iraq.

Mr. Chairman, Congressman Lantos, and other members of the committee, you and I have been discussing Iraq for many years. In fact, many of the committee members go back to the days before the Gulf War when I came up and testified on so many occasions about what we were doing in that buildup of Desert Shield.

We all remember vividly that in 1990, Saddam Hussein's forces, as both of you have noted, invaded Kuwait, brutalized that population, and at that time rejected the international community's ultimatum to withdraw.

The United States built a worldwide coalition—we got the whole international community involved at that time—with the clear political purpose of liberating Kuwait. And the military instrument of that coalition, led by America, had an equally clear military objective that flowed directly from the political purpose, and that was to eject the Iraqi army out of Kuwait.

The United Nations Security Council endorsed this purpose and objective, and the international community responded with unprecedented political backing, financial support, and military forces. And as a result, we not only accomplished our mission in the Gulf War, the way in which we did it was a model of American leadership and a model of international cooperation.

When the war ended, the Security Council of the United Nations agreed to take measures to ensure that Iraq did not threaten any of its neighbors again. Saddam Hussein, as you all both have noted and all will note, was a man after all who had sent his armies against Iran in 1980 and then against Kuwait in 1990, who had fired ballistic missiles at neighboring countries, and who had used chemical weapons in the war with Iran and even against his own people. The United States and the international community at that time were strongly determined to prevent any future aggression.

So United Nations Security Council Resolution 687 of 3 April 1991 fixed the terms of the cease-fire in the Gulf. And the fundamental purpose of this resolution and many more that followed was restoration of regional peace and security by way of a series of stringent demands on Iraq, particularly its disarmament with respect to weapons of mass destruction and possession of ballistic missiles with ranges greater than 150 kilometers. Desert Storm had dramatically reduced Iraq's more conventional military capability while at the same time not leaving Iraq so prostrate that it could not defend itself against Iran. It just had finished a war with Iran, and we did not want to give Iran an opportunity to start that war up again from a position of superiority. The focus of 687 was on weapons of mass destruction, and the resolutions that followed focused on that and other problems with Iraq that I will touch on in a moment.

Mr. Chairman, members of the committee, you know the rest of the story. You heard the president relate it at the United Nations seven days ago today. Iraq has defied the United Nations and refused to comply completely with any of the United Nations Security Council Resolutions that were passed. Moreover, since December of 1998 when the United Nations inspection teams left Iraq because of the regime's flagrant defiance of the UN, the Iraqi regime, Saddam Hussein, has been free to pursue weapons of mass destruction.

Meanwhile, the world has changed dramatically.

Since September 11, 2001, the world is a different place, a more dangerous place than the place that existed before September 11 or a few years ago when the inspectors were last in. As a consequence of the terrorist attacks on that day and of the war on terrorism that those attacks made necessary, a new reality was born: The world had to recognize that the potential connection between terrorists and weapons of mass destruction moved terrorism to a new level of threat, a threat that could not be deterred, as has been

---

A proven menace like Saddam Hussein, in possession of weapons of mass destruction, could empower a few terrorists to threaten millions of innocent people.

---

noted; a threat that we could not allow to grow because of this connection between states developing weapons of mass destruction and terrorist organizations willing to use them without any compunction and in an undeterrable fashion. In fact, that nexus became the overriding security concern of our nation. It still is and will continue to be so for years to come.

We now see that a proven menace like Saddam Hussein, in possession of weapons of mass destruction, could empower a few terrorists to threaten millions of innocent people.

President Bush is fully determined to deal with this threat. This administration is determined to defeat it. I believe the American people would have us do no less.

President Bush is also aware of the need to engage the international community. Just as an earlier President Bush did some 12 years ago, he understands perfectly how powerful a strong and unified international community can be, as we have seen so well-demonstrated in the war on terrorism in Afghanistan and elsewhere, a war on terrorism that is each day producing new successes, one step, one arrest, one apprehension at a time.

The need to engage the international community is why the president took his message on the grave and gathering danger of Iraq to the United Nations last week. Moreover, it is the United Nations that is the offended party, not Iraq, as some people might claim. Not just the United States, it is the international community that should be offended.

> *Once inspectors began to operate, Iraq continued to do everything to frustrate their work.*

It is a combination of United Nations resolutions that have been systematically and brutally ignored and violated for these past 12 years. It was United Nations inspectors who found it impossible to do their job and had to leave the work unfinished.

The president's challenge to the United Nations General Assembly was a direct one and it was a very simple one: If you would remain relevant, you must act. You must not look away from this challenge.

The president's speech was powerful. I was there. I listened to it. I knew what he was going to say, and I could see the energy in the room as he delivered it. It energized the United Nations General Assembly and it energized the debate taking place at this 57th meeting of the United Nations General Assembly. It changed the political landscape on which this issue was being discussed. It made it clear that Iraq is the problem. Iraq is the one that is in material breach of the demands placed on it by this multilateral organization, the United Nations.

The president made clear what was expected of Iraq was to repair this breach if they could. He made it clear that the issue, however, was more than just disarming Iraq by eliminating its weapons of mass destruction and by constraining its mid- and long-range missile capability. The UN resolutions also spoke of terrorism, human rights, the return of prisoners, the return of property, and the proper use of the Oil-for-Food program. And the indictment that the president laid out didn't need much discussion or debate. Everybody sitting in that chamber last Thursday knew that Iraq stood guilty of the charges. It convicted itself by its action over these past 12 years. There can be no question that Iraq is in material breach of its obligations.

Over the past weekend while I worked the aftermath of the President's speech, I saw the pressure build on Iraq as the Arab League, the secretary-general, and so many other nations pressed Iraq on the need to take action because it stood guilty and nobody could deny the guilt.

And four days ago, on Monday, Iraq responded not with a serious offer but with a familiar, tactical ploy to try to get out of the box, to try to get out of the corner once more. The Iraqi foreign minister said Iraq would let the inspectors in "without conditions." And this morning, in a speech at the United Nations he challenged President Bush's September 12th speech. He even called for a discussion of the issue of inspection teams in accordance "with international law." He is already walking back. He is already stepping away from the

"without conditions" statement they made on Monday. But he is not deceiving anybody. It is a ploy we have seen before. We have seen it on many occasions. And on each occasion, once inspectors began to operate, Iraq continued to do everything to frus-
trate their work.

There is absolutely no reason to expect that Iraq has changed.

Mr. Chairman, I will call your attention and the members' attention to the written statement that I have submitted, and I ask that it be put in the record, where I record a dozen examples of Iraq's defiance of the UN mandate. Cited in that longer statement is everything from intimidation at gunpoint to holding up inspectors while all the incriminating evidence was removed from the site to be inspected. It is a litany of defiance, unscrupulous behavior, and every sort of attempt at noncompliance. And by no means have I listed everything, only a sampling.

The Iraqi regime is infamous for its ploys, stalling tactics, its demands on inspectors, sometimes at the point of a gun, and its general and consistent defiance of the mandate of the United Nations Security Council. There is absolutely no reason to expect that Iraq has changed, that this latest effort of theirs to welcome inspectors without conditions is not just another ploy.

Let's be absolutely clear about the reason for their announcement Monday and what their foreign minister said today. They did not suddenly see the error of their ways. They did not suddenly want to clear up the problems of the past 12 years. They were responding to the heat and the pressure generated by the international community after President Bush's speech.

The United States has made it clear to our Security Council colleagues that we will not fall for this ploy. This is the time not to welcome what they said and become giddy, as some have done. This is the time to apply even more pressure. We must not relent. We must not believe that inspectors going in under the same conditions that caused their withdrawal four years ago is in any way acceptable or will bring us to a solution to this problem. These four years have been more than enough for Iraq to procure, develop, and hide proscribed items well beyond the reach of the kinds of inspections that were subject to Saddam's cheat and retreat approach from 1991 to 1998.

If inspectors do go back in because the UN feels it is appropriate for them to do so, they must go back in under a new regime with new rules, without any conditions, and without any opportunity for Iraq to frustrate their efforts.

It is up now to the United Nations Security Council to decide what action is required of Iraq to deal with this material breach of the United Nations mandate. If part of that solution that the Security Council comes to involves an inspection regime, it must be a regime that goes in with the authority of a new resolution that removes the weaknesses of the present regime and which will not tolerate any Iraqi disobedience. It cannot be a resolution that will be negotiated with Iraq. The resolution must be strong enough and comprehensive enough that it produces disarmament, and not just inspections.

Many United Nation members, including some on the Security Council, want to take Iraq at its word and send inspectors back in without any new resolution or new authority. It's a recipe for failure, and we will not support that. The debate we have begun to have within the council is on the need for and the wording of a resolution. Our position is clear: we must face the facts and find Iraq in material breach, then we must specify the actions we demand of Iraq, which President Bush has already laid out in his speech last week.

And then here's the key element. Here's what will make it different from what we did in the past, and this must be an essential element of any road going forward, any plan to go forward from the Security Council. We must determine what consequences this time will flow from Iraq's failure to take action. That is what makes this different. This time, unlike any time over the previous 12 years of Iraqi defiance, there must be hard consequences. This time Iraq must comply with the UN mandate or there will be decisive action to compel compliance.

We will listen to other points of view and we'll try to reach agreement within the council. It will be a difficult debate. We will also preserve at all times the president of the United States' authority and ability to defend our nation and our interest, as he sees fit—do it with our friends, do it with the United Nations, or do it alone. But the president has made it clear that this is a problem that must be solved and will be solved.

Some have suggested that there is a conflict in this approach, that U.S. interests should be our total concern. But Mr. Chairman, both of these issues, both multilateral and unilateral, are important. We are a member of the United Nations Security Council. We are a member of the United Nations. It is a multilateral institution whose resolutions have been violated. But the United States, as a separate matter, believes that its interests are threatened even if the United Nations has not continued to come to that conclusion.

We are trying to solve this problem through the United Nations and in a multilateral way. The president took the case to the UN because it is the body that should deal with such matters as Iraq. It was created to deal with such matters. President Bush is hoping that the UN will act in a decisive way. But at the same time, as he has made clear, and my other colleagues in the administration have made clear and I make clear today, if the United Nations is not able to act and act decisively—and I think that would be a terrible indictment of the UN—then the United States will have to make its own decision as to whether the danger posed by Iraq is such that we have to act in order to defend our country and to defend our interests.

And Mr. Chairman, our diplomatic efforts at the United Nations would be helped by a strong, strong congressional resolution authorizing President Bush to take action. The president should be authorized to use all means he determines appropriate, including military force, to enforce the United Nations Security Council resolutions that Iraq is defying and to defend the United States and its interests against the threat Iraq poses and to restore international peace and security to the region.

I know that the administration has provided language to the Congress. I ask that the Congress consider it carefully and quickly, and I ask for immediate action on such a resolution to show the world that the United States is united in this effort. To help the United Nations understand the seriousness of this issue, it would be important for all of us to speak as a nation, as a country, and to give this powerful signal to our diplomatic efforts in the United Nations.

Mr. Chairman, my colleagues in the intelligence community and my colleague, Secretary Rumsfeld, are giving the Congress additional information with respect to military ideas and options, with respect to the intelligence supporting the conclusions we have come to. So I will not take any time to do that here today, but I am prepared to answer any questions in these areas that you think I might be competent and qualified to answer.

But let me say this about the Iraq threat before I stop and allow the greater part of our time available for your important questions to be answered. We can have debates, discussions, and disagreements about the size and nature of the Iraqi stockpile of weapons of mass destruction, and we can discuss whether they are or are not violating the range constraints on the missiles that they have. But no one can doubt the record of Iraqi violations of United Nations Security Council resolutions. That is not debatable. It's a fact. It's a stated fact.

And no one can doubt Iraq's intention to continue to try to get these weapons of mass destruction unless they are stopped, and that is also not debatable. And I hope that will help to shape our debate and our discussions and the important decisions that we may have to make as a nation. These two realities—their intention and their continued violations over time—are indisputable.

With that, Mr. Chairman, I will stop and look forward to the questions from the committee. And once again, I ask that my full statement be put in the record.

Eliminating the Threat: The Right Course of Action for Disarming Iraq, Combating Terrorism, Protecting the Homeland, and Stabilizing the Middle East[2]

Edward M. Kennedy

U.S. senator from Massachusetts, 1962– ; born Boston, MA, February 22, 1932; served in army, 1951–53; B.A. in government, Harvard University, 1956; attended International Law School, The Hague (Netherlands), 1958; LL.B., University of Virginia, 1959; assistant district attorney, Suffolk County, MA, 1961–62; elected to U.S. Senate, 1962, to finish the term of his brother, John F. Kennedy; second-most senior member of the Senate; senior Democrat on the Health, Education, Labor, and Pensions Committee; member of the Judiciary Committee and the Armed Services Committee; sponsored Health Insurance Program, 1997; trustee, John F. Kennedy Center for the Performing Arts.

Editors' introduction: On September 19, 2002, President Bush proposed to Congress a resolution that authorized him "to use all means that he determines appropriate, including force, in order to enforce the United Nations Security Council Resolutions . . . , defend the national security interests of the United States against the threat posed by Iraq, and restore international peace and security in the region." Concerned that leaders of both parties in Congress were rushing to support the president's initiatives, Senator Kennedy told an audience convened at the Johns Hopkins Paul H. Nitze School of Advanced International Studies that "the life and death issue of war and peace is too important to be left to politics." The Nitze School was begun to train men and women in international affairs during the post–World War II era and continues to provide rigorous training in the area of international relations. He was introduced by the historian Francis Fukuyama.

Edward M. Kennedy's speech: Thank you, Dr. Fukuyama for that generous introduction.

---

2. Delivered September 27, 2002, the first floor of the school's Nitze Building, at 11 A.M., Washington, D.C.

I'm honored to be here at the School of Advanced International Studies. Many of the most talented individuals in foreign policy have benefitted immensely from your outstanding graduate program, and I welcome the opportunity to meet with you today.

I have come here today to express my view that America should not go to war against Iraq unless and until other reasonable alternatives are exhausted. But I begin with the strongest possible affirmation that good and decent people on all sides of this debate, who may in the end stand on opposing sides of this decision, are equally committed to our national security.

> *It is possible to love America while concluding that it is not now wise to go to war.*

The life and death issue of war and peace is too important to be left to politics. And I disagree with those who suggest that this fateful issue cannot or should not be contested vigorously, publicly, and all across America. When it is the people's sons and daughters who will risk and even lose their lives, then the people should hear and be heard, speak and be listened to.

But there is a difference between honest public dialogue and partisan appeals. There is a difference between questioning policy and questioning motives. There are Republicans and Democrats who support the immediate use of force—and Republicans and Democrats who have raised doubts and dissented.

In this serious time for America and many American families, no one should poison the public square by attacking the patriotism of opponents, or by assailing proponents as more interested in the cause of politics than in the merits of their cause. I reject this, as should we all.

Let me say it plainly: I not only concede, but I am convinced that President Bush believes genuinely in the course he urges upon us. And let me say with the same plainness: Those who agree with that course have an equal obligation—to resist any temptation to convert patriotism into politics. It is possible to love America while concluding that it is not now wise to go to war. The standard that should guide us is especially clear when lives are on the line: We must ask what is right for country and not party.

That is the true spirit of September 11—not unthinking unanimity, but a clear-minded unity in our determination to defeat terrorism—to defend our values and the value of life itself.

Just a year ago, the American people and the Congress rallied behind the president and our armed forces as we went to war in Afghanistan. Al Qaeda and the Taliban protectors who gave them sanctuary in Afghanistan posed a clear, present, and continuing danger. The need to destroy Al Qaeda was urgent and undeniable.

In the months that followed September 11, the Bush administration marshaled an international coalition. Today, 90 countries are enlisted in the effort, from providing troops to providing law enforcement, intelligence, and other critical support.

> ***Resorting to war is not America's only or best course at this juncture.***

But I am concerned that using force against Iraq before other means are tried will sorely test both the integrity and effectiveness of the coalition. Just one year into the campaign against Al Qaeda, the administration is shifting focus, resources, and energy to Iraq. The change in priority is coming before we have fully eliminated the threat from Al Qaeda, before we know whether Osama bin Laden is dead or alive, and before we can be assured that the fragile post-Taliban government in Afghanistan will consolidate its authority.

No one disputes that America has lasting and important interests in the Persian Gulf, or that Iraq poses a significant challenge to U.S. interests. There is no doubt that Saddam Hussein's regime is a serious danger, that he is a tyrant, and that his pursuit of lethal weapons of mass destruction cannot be tolerated. He must be disarmed.

How can we best achieve this objective in a way that minimizes the risks to our country? How can we ignore the danger to our young men and women in uniform, to our ally Israel, to regional stability, the international community, and victory against terrorism?

There is clearly a threat from Iraq, and there is clearly a danger, but the administration has not made a convincing case that we face such an imminent threat to our national security that a unilateral, pre-emptive American strike and an immediate war are necessary.

Nor has the administration laid out the cost in blood and treasure of this operation.

With all the talk of war, the administration has not explicitly acknowledged, let alone explained to the American people, the immense post-war commitment that will be required to create a stable Iraq.

The president's challenge to the United Nations requires a renewed effort to enforce the will of the international community to disarm Saddam. Resorting to war is not America's only or best course at this juncture. There are realistic alternatives between doing nothing and declaring unilateral or immediate war. War should be a last resort, not the first response. Let us follow that course, and the world will be with us—even if, in the end, we have to move to the ultimate sanction of armed conflict.

The Bush administration says America can fight a war in Iraq without undermining our most pressing national security priority—the war against Al Qaeda. But I believe it is inevitable that a war in Iraq without serious international support will weaken our effort to ensure that Al Qaeda terrorists can never, never, never threaten American lives again.

Unfortunately, the threat from Al Qaeda is still imminent. The nation's armed forces and law enforcement are on constant high alert. America may have broken up the Al Qaeda network in Afghanistan and scattered its operatives across many lands. But we have not broken its will to kill Americans.

As I said earlier, we still don't know the fate, the location, or the operational capacity of Osama bin Laden himself. But we do know that Al Qaeda is still there, and still here in America—and will do all it can to strike at America's heart and heartland again. But we don't know when, where, or how this may happen.

On March 12, CIA Director Tenet testified before the Senate Armed Services Committee that Al Qaeda remains "the most immediate and serious threat" to our country, "despite the progress we have made in Afghanistan and in disrupting the network elsewhere."

Even with the Taliban out of power, Afghanistan remains fragile. Security remains tenuous. Warlords still dominate many regions. Our reconstruction effort, which is vital to long-term stability and security, is halting and inadequate. Some Al Qaeda operatives—no one knows how many—have faded into the general population. Terrorist attacks are on the rise. President Karzai, who has already survived one assassination attempt, is still struggling to solidify his hold on power. And although neighboring Pakistan has been our ally, its stability is far from certain.

We know all this—and we also know that it is an open secret in Washington that the nation's uniformed military leadership is skeptical about the wisdom of war with Iraq. They share the concern that it may adversely affect the ongoing war against Al Qaeda and the continuing effort in Afghanistan by draining resources and armed forces already stretched so thin that many reservists have been called for a second year of duty, and record numbers of service members have been kept on active duty beyond their obligated service.

To succeed in our global war against Al Qaeda and terrorism, the United States depends on military, law enforcement, and intelligence support from many other nations. We depend on Russia and countries in the former Soviet Union that border Afghanistan for military cooperation. We depend on countries from Portugal to Pakistan to the Philippines for information about Al Qaeda's plans and intentions. Because of these relationships, terrorist plots are being foiled and Al Qaeda operatives are being arrested. It is far from clear that these essential relationships will be able to survive the strain of a war with Iraq that comes before the alternatives are tried—or without the support of an international coalition.

A largely unilateral American war that is widely perceived in the Muslim world as untimely or unjust could worsen not lessen the threat of terrorism. War with Iraq before a genuine attempt at inspection and disarmament, or without genuine international support, could swell the ranks of Al Qaeda sympathizers and trigger an escalation in terrorist acts. As General Clark told the Senate Armed Services Committee, it would "super-charge recruiting for Al Qaeda."

General Hoar advised the committee on September 23 that America's first and primary effort should be to defeat Al Qaeda. In a September 10 article, General Clark wrote: "Unilateral U.S. action today would disrupt the war against Al Qaeda." We ignore such wisdom and advice from many of the best of our military at our own peril.

We have known for many years that Saddam Hussein is seeking and developing weapons of mass destruction. Our intelligence community is also deeply concerned about the acquisition of such weapons by Iran, North Korea, Libya, Syria, and other nations. But information from the intelligence community over the past six months does not point to Iraq as an imminent threat to the United States or a major proliferator of weapons of mass destruction.

There is no clear and convincing pattern of Iraqi relations with either Al Qaeda or the Taliban.

In public hearings before the Senate Armed Services Committee in March, CIA Director George Tenet described Iraq as a threat but not as a proliferator, saying that Saddam Hussein—and I quote—"is determined to thwart UN sanctions, press ahead with weapons of mass destruction, and resurrect the military force he had before the Gulf War." That is unacceptable, but it is also possible that it could be stopped short of war.

In recent weeks, in briefings and in hearings in the Senate Armed Services Committee, I have seen no persuasive evidence that Saddam would not be deterred from attacking U.S. interests by America's overwhelming military superiority.

I have heard no persuasive evidence that Saddam is on the threshold of acquiring the nuclear weapons he has sought for more than 20 years.

And the administration has offered no persuasive evidence that Saddam would transfer chemical or biological weapons of mass destruction to Al Qaeda or any other terrorist organization. As General Joseph Hoar, the former commander of Central Command told the members of the Armed Services Committee, a case has not been made to connect Al Qaeda and Iraq.

To the contrary, there is no clear and convincing pattern of Iraqi relations with either Al Qaeda or the Taliban.

General Wesley Clark, former supreme allied commander Europe, testified before the Armed Services Committee on September 23 that Iran has had closer ties to terrorism than Iraq. Iran has a nuclear weapons development program, and it already has a missile that can reach Israel.

Moreover, in August, former National Security Adviser Brent Scowcroft wrote that there is "scant evidence" linking Saddam Hussein to terrorist organizations and "even less to the September 11 attacks." He concluded that Saddam would not regard it as in his interest to risk his country or his investment in weapons of mass destruction by transferring them to terrorists who would use them and "leave Baghdad as the return address."

At the present time, we do face a pressing risk of proliferation—from Russia's stockpile of weapons of mass destruction. America spends only $1 billion a year to safeguard those weapons. Yet the administration is preparing to spend between one and two hundred billion dollars on a war with Iraq.

I do not accept the idea that trying other alternatives is either futile or perilous—that the risks of waiting are greater than the risks of war. Indeed, in launching a war against Iraq now, the United States may precipitate the very threat that we are intent on preventing—weapons of mass destruction in the hands of terrorists. If Saddam's regime and his very survival are threatened, then his view of his interests may be profoundly altered: He may decide he has nothing to lose by using weapons of mass destruction himself or by sharing them with terrorists.

Some who advocate military action against Iraq, however, assert that air strikes will do the job quickly and decisively, and that the operation will be complete in 72 hours. But there is again no persuasive evidence that air strikes alone over the course of several days will incapacitate Saddam and destroy his weapons of mass destruction. Experts have informed us that we do not have sufficient intelligence about military targets in Iraq. Saddam may well hide his most lethal weapons in mosques, schools, and hospitals. If our forces attempt to strike such targets, untold numbers of Iraqi civilians could be killed.

In the Gulf War, many of Saddam's soldiers quickly retreated because they did not believe the invasion of Kuwait was justified. But when Iraq's survival is at stake, it is more likely that they will fight to the end. Saddam and his military may well abandon the desert, retreat to Baghdad, and engage in urban, guerrilla warfare.

In our September 23 hearing, General Clark told the committee that we would need a large military force and a plan for urban warfare. General Hoar said that our military would have to be prepared to fight block by block in Baghdad, and that we could lose a battalion of soldiers a day in casualties. Urban fighting would, he said, look like the last brutal 15 minutes of the movie *Saving Private Ryan*.

Before the Gulf War in 1991, Secretary of State James Baker met with the Iraqis and threatened Hussein with "catastrophe" if he employed weapons of mass destruction. In that war, although Saddam launched 39 Scud missiles at Israel, he did not use the chemical or biological weapons he had.

If Saddam's regime and survival are threatened, he will have nothing to lose, and may use everything at his disposal. Israeli prime minister Ariel Sharon has announced that instead of its forbearance in the 1991 Gulf War, this time Israel will respond if attacked. If weapons of mass destruction land on Israeli soil, killing innocent civilians, the experts I have consulted believe Israel will retaliate, and possibly with nuclear weapons.

This escalation, spiraling out of control, could draw the Arab world into a regional war in which our Arab allies side with Iraq, against the United States and against Israel. And that would represent a fundamental threat to Israel, to the region, to the world economy and international order.

Nor can we rule out the possibility that Saddam would assault American forces with chemical or biological weapons. Despite advances in protecting our troops, we do not yet have the capability to safeguard all of them.

Our soldiers, sailors, airmen, and marines are serving their country with great distinction. Just under 70,000 reservists and National Guardsmen have been mobilized for the war against terrorism. If we embark upon a premature or unilateral military campaign against Iraq, or a campaign only with Britain, our forces will

---

War is the last resort. If in the end we have to take that course, the burden should be shared with allies.

---

have to serve in even greater numbers, for longer periods, and with graver risks. Our force strength will be stretched even thinner. And war is the last resort. If in the end we have to take that course, the burden should be shared with allies—and that is less likely if war becomes an immediate response.

Even with the major technological gains demonstrated in Afghanistan, the logistics of such a war would be extraordinarily challenging if we could not marshal a real coalition of regional and international allies.

President Bush made the right decision on September 12 when he expressed America's willingness to work with the United Nations to prevent Iraq from using chemical, biological, or nuclear weapons. The president's address to the General Assembly challenging the United Nations to enforce its long list of Security Council Resolutions on Iraq was powerful—and for me, it was persuasive.

But to maintain the credibility he built when he went to the UN, the president must follow the logic of his own argument.

Before we go to war, we should give the international community the chance to meet the president's challenge—to renew its resolve to disarm Saddam Hussein completely and effectively. This makes the resumption of inspections more imperative and perhaps more likely than at any time since they ended in 1998.

So this should be the first aim of our policy—to get UN inspectors back into Iraq without conditions. I hope the Security Council will approve a new resolution requiring the Government of Iraq to accept unlimited and unconditional inspections and the destruction of any weapons of mass destruction.

The resolution should set a short timetable for the resumption of inspections. I would hope that inspections could resume, at the latest, by the end of October.

The resolution should also require the head of the UN inspection team to report to the Security Council every two weeks. No delaying tactics should be tolerated—and if they occur, Saddam should know that he will lose his last chance to avoid war.

The Security Council Resolution should authorize the use of force, if the inspection process is unsatisfactory. And there should be no doubt in Baghdad that the United States Congress would then be prepared to authorize force as well.

The return of inspectors with unfettered access and the ability to destroy what they find not only could remove any weapons of mass destruction from Saddam's arsenal, they could also be more effective than an immediate or unilateral war in ensuring that these deadly weapons would not fall into terrorist hands.

The seven years of inspections that took place until 1998 succeeded in virtually eliminating Saddam's ability to develop a nuclear weapon in Iraq during that period. Even with Iraq's obstructions, those inspections resulted in the demolition of large quantities of chemical and biological weapons. By the time the inspectors were forced out of the country in 1998, they had accomplished far more disarmament than the Gulf War itself. And before going to war again, we should seek to resume the inspections now—and set a nonnegotiable demand of no obstruction, no delay, no more weapons of mass destruction in Iraq.

What can be gained here is success—and in the event of failure, greater credibility for an armed response, greater international support, and the prospect of victory with less loss of American life.

So what is to be lost by pursuing this policy before Congress authorizes sending young Americans into another and in this case perhaps unnecessary war?

Even the case against Saddam is, in important respects, a case against immediate or unilateral war. If Prime Minister Blair is correct in saying that Iraq can launch chemical or biological warheads in 45 minutes, what kind of sense does it make to put our soldiers in the path of that danger without exhausting every reasonable means to disarm Iraq through the United Nations?

Clearly we must halt Saddam Hussein's quest for weapons of mass destruction. Yes, we may reach the point where our only choice is conflict—with like-minded allies at our side, if not in a multilateral action authorized by the Security Council. But we are not there yet.

The evidence does not take us there; events do not compel us there—and both the war against terrorism and our wider interests in the region and the world summon us to a course that is sensible, graduated, and genuinely strong—not because it moves swiftly to battle, but because it moves resolutely to the objective of disarming Iraq—peacefully if possible, and militarily if necessary.

Let me close by recalling the events of an autumn of danger four decades ago. When missiles were discovered in Cuba—missiles more threatening to us than anything Saddam has today—some in the highest councils of government urged an immediate and unilateral strike. Instead the United States took its case to the United Nations, won the endorsement of the Organization of American States, and brought along even our most skeptical allies. We imposed a blockade, demanded inspection, and insisted on the removal of the missiles.

When an earlier president outlined that choice to the American people and the world, he spoke of it in realistic terms—not with a sense that the first step would necessarily be the final step, but with a resolve that it must be tried.

As he said then, "Action is required . . . and these actions [now] may only be the beginning. We will not prematurely or unnecessarily risk the costs of . . . war—but neither will we shrink from that risk at any time it must be faced."

In 2002, we too can and must be both resolute and measured. In that way, the United States prevailed without war in the greatest confrontation of the cold war. Now, on Iraq, let us build international support, try the United Nations, and pursue disarmament before we turn to armed conflict.

Allies Working Toward a Secure Future

Don't Position USA as "Common Enemy" in Volatile Region[3]

Marcy Kaptur

Member U.S. House of Representatives, Ninth Ohio District, 1983– ; born Toledo, OH, June 17, 1946; B.A. in history, University of Wisconsin, 1968; master's degree in urban planning, University of Michigan, 1974; post-graduate, University of Manchester (England), 1974; assistant director of urban affairs and domestic policy staff, White House, 1977–79; served on House committees of Appropriations, Veterans Affairs, Budget, Banking, Finance and Urban Affairs, and subcommittees on Agriculture, Housing and Urban Development, Environmental Protection, NASA, and the National Science Foundation; author, Women in Congress *(1996); honorary doctor of laws, University of Toledo; "Legislator of the Year," by National Mental Health Association; Ellis Island Medal of Honor, 2002.*

Editors' introduction: After terrorists killed thousands of persons in New York City, Washington, D.C., and Shanksville, Pennsylvania, on September 11, 2001, elected officials in the Capitol debated what should be done to prevent further attacks. On September 19, 2002, President Bush proposed to Congress a resolution authorizing him "to use all means that he determines to be appropriate, including force" against Iraq. Less than a month later, Representative Kaptur warned that the administration was "positioning the U.S. to be the common enemy in a volatile region where terrorism grows with each passing decade of war and remembrance."

Marcy Kaptur's speech: To achieve long-term stability, U.S. policy toward the Arab and Islamic world must be shaped multilaterally and affirm our nation's belief in democratic principles. The Bush administration's initiatives will lead to neither. Indeed, it is positioning the U.S. to be the common enemy in a volatile region where terrorism grows with each passing decade of war and remembrance.

---

3. Delivered October 3, 2002, on the floor of the U.S. House of Representatives, Washington, D.C.

Bush policies—such as threatening regime change or the "one bullet policy" on Iraq—are destabilizing and pose a real threat to U.S. long-term interests. These irresponsible policies inject the U.S. into the festering antipathy of disparate forces whose common denominator is growing anti-Western sentiment.

> *If America goes to war, the cause must be just and better justified.*

Thus, a resolution that employs all diplomatic and economic means to draw broad multilateral support to allow UN arms inspectors access to conduct robust investigations of Iraq's suspected weapons sites is of paramount importance. As a first step, Congress should support the recently negotiated international agreement allowing inspectors to return to Iraq after four years. Especially in this region of the world, former Senator George Mitchell emphasizes the importance of diplomacy in the Mitchell Report, "Whatever the source, violence will not solve the problems of the region. It will only make them worse. Death and destruction will not bring peace, but will deepen the hatred and harden the resolve on both sides. There is only one way to peace, justice, and security in the Middle East, and that is through negotiation."

First Strike

Based on the lack of verifiable evidence presented to Congress and the American people, the president's proposal to pre-emptively, or unilaterally, strike against Iraq is unacceptable. Due to the predictably destabilizing effect on the region, the U.S. should avoid a first strike. Dr. Mark Juergensmeyer, director of Global and International Studies at U.C. Santa Barbara, said "It is essential that a multilateral force be deployed if action is contemplated."

If America goes to war, the cause must be just and better justified.

Toward a Changed Region

Powerful Islamic stirrings inside undemocratic regimes in the Middle East and Central Asia, including violent forces operating outside nation-states (like Al Qaeda), create conditions for emerging revolutions. In responding to these, the U.S. must act in a manner that is true to our founding principles as the world's oldest democratic republic. We, too, have been a revolutionary people aspiring to a better way of life.

We must not wed ourselves to monarchy, dictatorship, or repression. As a superpower, the U.S. must position itself for long-term relations with many emerging nations. The U.S. should not become the inheritor of a new world order in the Middle East and Central Asia, nor an occupying force. Simply put, U.S. dominance there is not unilaterally sustainable.

Grave and Gathering vs. Imminent Threat

Congress must ask: What is the "imminent threat" to the U.S. that justifies a war resolution now? The president, in his remarks before the UN, stated, "Iraq is a grave and gathering danger." He did not say "an imminent threat."

What has Iraq done differently in the last 4 months than the prior year to warrant invasion now? Yes, Iraq

> *For how long will Americans be asked to die for "vital interests" centered in the oil kingdoms?*

is a secular state that seeks greater domination over the Arab world. But intelligence briefings have indicated that Iraq has fewer military capabilities than it did 10 years ago. Secretary Rumsfeld has stated that Iraq's army is only 40 percent of what it was 10 years ago. The Central Intelligence Agency and Defense Intelligence Agency have verified that Iraq's chemical and nuclear capabilities are substantially less than 10 years ago. However, in the area of biologics, Iraq is likely ahead of where it was 10 years ago.

The international community has the opportunity to use its united efforts to require Iraq to abide by UN resolutions requiring immediate access to verify Iraq's commitment to rid itself of weapons of mass destruction and long-range missiles.

There Is a Distinction Between Al Qaeda and Iraq

Congress must ask the Bush administration to distinguish between Al Qaeda and Iraq. The carnage that took place on September 11, 2001, was committed by members of the Al Qaeda terrorist network. Al Qaeda's primary objective is to rid the Middle East of all foreign influence and impose strict Islamic religious rule based on its particular interpretation of the religion. Iraq, rather, is a secular state headed by a military dictator, Saddam Hussein, holding the second largest oil reserves in the Middle East. Saddam's chief objective is to control the entire region's oil reserves and eventually gain greater power in the Arab world.

America's war on terrorism began as a clear campaign against Al Qaeda, not Iraq. Neither Congress nor the American public has been presented with any evidence of a connection between Iraq and Al Qaeda. Though some terrorists may be "present" especially in the northern zone of Iraq, which Hussein does not control, there is no linkage of evidence between them and the government of Iraq. The president asserted in his draft resolution that members of Al Qaeda are "known to be in Iraq" and that Iraq may give weapons to terrorists. His statements are filled with innuendos, not facts. No intelligence information has been presented to Congress to add certainty to the president's statements.

Oil Is the Primary Underpinning of U.S. "Vital" Interest

Congress must ask: For how long will Americans be asked to die for "vital interests" centered in the oil kingdoms? The economic underpinning of Iraq is oil—the second largest reserves in the world. Ninety-five percent of Iraq's economy is oil driven. Americans might ask the question: "Why has the U.S. become bogged down in this region so many times in modern history?" and "Why have all of America's major recessions in the past 30 years been triggered by rising oil prices?" In fact, rising oil prices triggered our current recession, and prices are rising again.

During the 1970s, two Arab oil embargoes drove the U.S. economy into deep recession. President Jimmy Carter tried to move America toward energy independence, calling the challenge the "moral equivalent of war." But as world oil prices dropped through O.P.E.C. price manipulation, America lost its edge on energy independence. Though conservation and alternative energy development progressed, their pace was not sufficient to meet demand.

> *America needs a national commitment to become energy independent again in this decade.*

In the early 1990s, America went to war over Iraq's invasion of neighboring Kuwait's oil fields and port access. In October 2000, the USS *Cole*, a Navy destroyer protecting the oil shipping lanes in the Persian Gulf, was suicide bombed in Yemen's harbor. Even now, as the president contemplates invasion, 8 percent of America's oil originates in Iraq.

Oil is not worth one more American soldier's life, nor any more disruption to our national economy. America needs a national commitment to become energy independent again in this decade, much like the space program of the 1960s that led America into the heavens. Ms. Robin Wright, foreign diplomatic correspondent for the *Los Angeles Times*, has stated, "To build a more peaceful world, the U.S. must deal with the oil issue. It must also deal with the political destiny of people in that part of the world who want to have some say in their futures."

Naked Aggression Is Not the American Way

Yes, Iraq is in gross violation of UN resolutions calling for inspections, but America should not pressure Iraq unilaterally, without maintaining that same broad-based international support. It was proper for President Bush to deliver an address at the United Nations. Our nation has always sought to be a constructive partner among the community of nations. We need to maintain this policy of engagement with the nations of the world.

Naked aggression by a superpower with no evidence presented to its lawmakers is discomforting to the American people and not the way to forge alliances in a troubled part of the world. America, surely, does not wish to be perceived as the "bully on the block" in the most oil rich region of the world where not one democratic state exists.

A Plan for the Future

As a first step, we should support International Strategic Partnership to Eliminate a Common Threat (INSPECT), an alternate resolution encouraging the president to support the recently negotiated inspection plan between the Iraqi government and international representatives calling for a robust team capable of ensuring that Iraq is no longer in violation of international agreements. The resolution rejects any unilateral military action by the U.S. until Congress is able to grant its approval. In addition, the president must submit a report to Congress, at least every 30 days, on matters relevant to this resolution. According to David Albright, president of the Institute for Science and International Security, "Nuclear threat is not imminent. Because the threat is not imminent, inspectors could be beneficial."

Remarks on Iraq[4]

George W. Bush

President of the United States, 2001– ; born New Haven, CT, July 6, 1946, and raised in Midland and Houston, TX; attended Phillips Academy, Andover, MA; B.A., Yale University; M.B.A., Harvard Business School, 1975; F-102 pilot, Texas Air National Guard, 1968–73; oil and gas business, Midland, TX, 1975–86; senior adviser in father's presidential campaign, 1987–88; one of the partners that purchased the Texas Rangers baseball franchise, 1989, and managing general partner of the team, 1989–1994; governor of Texas, 1995– 2000.

Editors' introduction: After thousands of people were killed by terrorist attacks in New York City, Washington, D.C., and Pennsylvania on September 11, 2001, in an address on September 20 of that year, President Bush promised the Congress and the American people that "our war" would "not end . . . until every terrorist group of global reach has been found, stopped, and defeated." In carrying out this pledge, Mr. Bush first sent troops to Afghanistan and then turned his attention to Iraq. On September 19, 2002, he proposed to Congress a resolution authorizing him to use force, if necessary, "to enforce the United Nations Security Council Resolutions . . . , defend the national security interests of the United States against the threat posed by Iraq, and restore international peace and security in the region." In the speech below, the president discussed what he perceived to be Iraq's "grave threat to peace and America's determination to lead the world in confronting that threat."

George W. Bush's speech: Thank you all. Thank you for that very gracious and warm Cincinnati welcome. I'm honored to be here tonight; I appreciate you all coming.

Tonight I want to take a few minutes to discuss a grave threat to peace, and America's determination to lead the world in confronting that threat.

The threat comes from Iraq. It arises directly from the Iraqi regime's own actions—its history of aggression and its drive toward an arsenal of terror. Eleven years ago, as a condition for ending the Persian Gulf War, the Iraqi regime was required to destroy its weapons of mass destruction, to cease all development of such weapons, and to stop all support for terrorist groups. The Iraqi regime

---

4. Delivered October 7, 2002, 8:02 P.M. EDT, at the Cincinatti Museum Center–Cincinatti Union Terminal, Cincinatti, OH.

has violated all of those obligations. It possesses and produces chemical and biological weapons. It is seeking nuclear weapons. It has given shelter and support to terrorism and practices terror against its own people. The entire world has witnessed Iraq's eleven-year history of defiance, deception, and bad faith.

We also must never forget the most vivid events of recent history. On September the 11th, 2001, America felt its vulnerability—even to threats that gather on the other side of the earth. We resolved then, and we are resolved today, to confront every threat, from any source, that could bring sudden terror and suffering to America.

Members of the Congress of both political parties, and members of the United Nations Security Council, agree that Saddam Hussein is a threat to peace and must disarm. We agree that the Iraqi dictator must not be permitted to threaten America and the world with horrible poisons and diseases and gases and atomic weapons. Since we all agree on this goal, the issue is: How can we best achieve it?

The entire world has witnessed Iraq's eleven-year history of defiance, deception, and bad faith.

Many Americans have raised legitimate questions: about the nature of the threat; about the urgency of action—why be concerned now; about the link between Iraq developing weapons of terror and the wider war on terror. These are all issues we've discussed broadly and fully within my administration. And tonight, I want to share those discussions with you.

First, some ask why Iraq is different from other countries or regimes that also have terrible weapons. While there are many dangers in the world, the threat from Iraq stands alone—because it gathers the most serious dangers of our age in one place. Iraq's weapons of mass destruction are controlled by a murderous tyrant who has already used chemical weapons to kill thousands of people. This same tyrant has tried to dominate the Middle East, has invaded and brutally occupied a small neighbor, has struck other nations without warning, and holds an unrelenting hostility toward the United States.

By its past and present actions, by its technological capabilities, by the merciless nature of its regime, Iraq is unique. As a former chief weapons inspector of the UN has said, "The fundamental problem with Iraq remains the nature of the regime itself. Saddam Hussein is a homicidal dictator who is addicted to weapons of mass destruction."

Some ask how urgent this danger is to America and the world. The danger is already significant, and it only grows worse with time. If we know Saddam Hussein has dangerous weapons today—and we do—does it make any sense for the world to wait to confront him as he grows even stronger and develops even more dangerous weapons?

In 1995, after several years of deceit by the Iraqi regime, the head of Iraq's military industries defected. It was then that the regime was forced to admit that it had produced more than 30,000 liters of anthrax and other deadly biological agents. The inspectors, however, concluded that Iraq had likely produced two to four times that amount. This is a massive stockpile of biological weapons that has never been accounted for, and capable of killing millions.

> *Over the years, Iraq has provided safe haven to terrorists.*

We know that the regime has produced thousands of tons of chemical agents, including mustard gas, sarin nerve gas, VX nerve gas. Saddam Hussein also has experience in using chemical weapons. He has ordered chemical attacks on Iran, and on more than forty villages in his own country. These actions killed or injured at least 20,000 people, more than six times the number of people who died in the attacks of September the 11th.

And surveillance photos reveal that the regime is rebuilding facilities that it had used to produce chemical and biological weapons. Every chemical and biological weapon that Iraq has or makes is a direct violation of the truce that ended the Persian Gulf War in 1991. Yet, Saddam Hussein has chosen to build and keep these weapons despite international sanctions, UN demands, and isolation from the civilized world.

Iraq possesses ballistic missiles with a likely range of hundreds of miles—far enough to strike Saudi Arabia, Israel, Turkey, and other nations—in a region where more than 135,000 American civilians and service members live and work. We've also discovered through intelligence that Iraq has a growing fleet of manned and unmanned aerial vehicles that could be used to disperse chemical or biological weapons across broad areas. We're concerned that Iraq is exploring ways of using these UAVs for missions targeting the United States. And, of course, sophisticated delivery systems aren't required for a chemical or biological attack; all that might be required are a small container and one terrorist or Iraqi intelligence operative to deliver it.

And that is the source of our urgent concern about Saddam Hussein's links to international terrorist groups. Over the years, Iraq has provided safe haven to terrorists such as Abu Nidal, whose terror organization carried out more than 90 terrorist attacks in 20 countries that killed or injured nearly 900 people, including 12 Americans. Iraq has also provided safe haven to Abu Abbas, who was responsible for seizing the *Achille Lauro* and killing an American passenger. And we know that Iraq is continuing to finance terror and gives assistance to groups that use terrorism to undermine Middle East peace.

We know that Iraq and the Al Qaeda terrorist network share a common enemy—the United States of America. We know that Iraq and Al Qaeda have had high-level contacts that go back a decade. Some Al Qaeda leaders who fled Afghanistan went to Iraq. These include one very senior Al Qaeda leader who received medical treatment in Baghdad this year, and who has been associated with planning for chemical and biological attacks. We've learned that Iraq has trained Al Qaeda members in bomb-making and poisons and deadly gases. And we know that after September the 11th, Saddam Hussein's regime gleefully celebrated the terrorist attacks on America.

Iraq could decide on any given day to provide a biological or chemical weapon to a terrorist group or individual terrorists. Alliance with terrorists could allow the Iraqi regime to attack America without leaving any fingerprints.

Some have argued that confronting the threat from Iraq could detract from the war against terror. To the contrary, confronting the threat posed by Iraq is crucial to winning the war on terror. When I spoke to Congress more than a year ago, I said that those who harbor terrorists are as guilty as the terrorists themselves. Saddam Hussein is harboring terrorists and the instruments of terror, the instruments of mass death and destruction. And he cannot be trusted. The risk is simply too great that he will use them, or provide them to a terror network.

Terror cells and outlaw regimes building weapons of mass destruction are different faces of the same evil. Our security requires that we confront both. And the United States military is capable of confronting both.

Many people have asked how close Saddam Hussein is to developing a nuclear weapon. Well, we don't know exactly, and that's the problem. Before the Gulf War, the best intelligence indicated that Iraq was eight to ten years away from developing a nuclear weapon. After the war, international inspectors learned that the regime has been much closer—the regime in Iraq would likely have possessed a nuclear weapon no later than 1993. The inspectors discovered that Iraq had an advanced nuclear weapons development program, had a design for a workable nuclear weapon, and was pursuing several different methods of enriching uranium for a bomb.

Before being barred from Iraq in 1998, the International Atomic Energy Agency dismantled extensive nuclear weapons–related facilities, including three uranium enrichment sites. That same year, information from a high-ranking Iraqi nuclear engineer who had defected revealed that despite his public promises, Saddam Hussein had ordered his nuclear program to continue.

The evidence indicates that Iraq is reconstituting its nuclear weapons program. Saddam Hussein has held numerous meetings with Iraqi nuclear scientists, a group he calls his "nuclear mujahideen"—his nuclear holy warriors. Satellite photographs reveal that Iraq is rebuilding facilities at sites that have been part of its nuclear program in the past. Iraq has attempted to purchase high-strength aluminum tubes and other equipment needed for gas centrifuges, which are used to enrich uranium for nuclear weapons.

If the Iraqi regime is able to produce, buy, or steal an amount of highly enriched uranium a little larger than a single softball, it could have a nuclear weapon in less than a year. And if we allow that to happen, a terrible line would be crossed. Saddam Hussein would be in a position to blackmail anyone who opposes his aggression. He would be in a position to dominate the Middle East. He would be in a position to threaten America. And Saddam Hussein would be in a position to pass nuclear technology to terrorists.

Some citizens wonder, after 11 years of living with this problem, why do we need to confront it now? And there's a reason. We've experienced the horror of September the 11th. We have seen that those who hate America are willing to crash airplanes into buildings full of innocent people. Our enemies would be no less willing—in fact, they would be eager—to use biological or chemical, or a nuclear weapon.

We cannot wait for the final proof—the smoking gun—that could come in the form of a mushroom cloud.

Knowing these realities, America must not ignore the threat gathering against us. Facing clear evidence of peril, we cannot wait for the final proof—the smoking gun—that could come in the form of a mushroom cloud. As President Kennedy said in October of 1962, "Neither the United States of America, nor the world community of nations can tolerate deliberate deception and offensive threats on the part of any nation, large or small. We no longer live in a world," he said, "where only the actual firing of weapons represents a sufficient challenge to a nation's security to constitute maximum peril."

Understanding the threats of our time, knowing the designs and deceptions of the Iraqi regime, we have every reason to assume the worst, and we have an urgent duty to prevent the worst from occurring.

Some believe we can address this danger by simply resuming the old approach to inspections, and applying diplomatic and economic pressure. Yet this is precisely what the world has tried to do since 1991. The UN inspections program was met with systematic deception. The Iraqi regime bugged hotel rooms and offices of inspectors to find where they were going next; they forged documents, destroyed evidence, and developed mobile weapons facilities to keep a step ahead of inspectors. Eight so-called presidential palaces were declared off-limits to unfettered inspections. These sites actually encompass twelve square miles, with hundreds of structures, both above and below the ground, where sensitive materials could be hidden.

The world has also tried economic sanctions—and watched Iraq use billions of dollars in illegal oil revenues to fund more weapons purchases, rather than providing for the needs of the Iraqi people.

The world has tried limited military strikes to destroy Iraq's weapons of mass destruction capabilities—only to see them openly rebuilt, while the regime again denies they even exist.

The world has tried no-fly zones to keep Saddam from terrorizing his own people—and in the last year alone, the Iraqi military has fired upon American and British pilots more than 750 times.

After eleven years during which we have tried containment, sanctions, inspections, even selected military action, the end result is that Saddam Hussein still has chemical and biological weapons and is increasing his capabilities to make more. And he is moving ever closer to developing a nuclear weapon.

Clearly, to actually work, any new inspections, sanctions, or enforcement mechanisms will have to be very different. America wants the UN to be an effective organization that helps keep the

---

The time for denying, deceiving, and delaying has come to an end.

---

peace. And that is why we are urging the Security Council to adopt a new resolution setting out tough, immediate requirements. Among those requirements: The Iraqi regime must reveal and destroy, under UN supervision, all existing weapons of mass destruction. To ensure that we learn the truth, the regime must allow witnesses to its illegal activities to be interviewed outside the country—and these witnesses must be free to bring their families with them so they are all beyond the reach of Saddam Hussein's terror and murder. And inspectors must have access to any site, at any time, without pre-clearance, without delay, without exceptions.

The time for denying, deceiving, and delaying has come to an end. Saddam Hussein must disarm himself—or, for the sake of peace, we will lead a coalition to disarm him.

Many nations are joining us in insisting that Saddam Hussein's regime be held accountable. They are committed to defending the international security that protects the lives of both our citizens and theirs. And that's why America is challenging all nations to take the resolutions of the UN Security Council seriously.

And these resolutions are clear. In addition to declaring and destroying all of its weapons of mass destruction, Iraq must end its support for terrorism. It must cease the persecution of its civilian population. It must stop all illicit trade outside the Oil For Food program. It must release or account for all Gulf War personnel, including an American pilot, whose fate is still unknown.

By taking these steps, and by only taking these steps, the Iraqi regime has an opportunity to avoid conflict. Taking these steps would also change the nature of the Iraqi regime

> ### *Failure to act would embolden other tyrants.*

itself. America hopes the regime will make that choice. Unfortunately, at least so far, we have little reason to expect it. And that's why two administrations—mine and President Clinton's—have stated that regime change in Iraq is the only certain means of removing a great danger to our nation.

I hope this will not require military action, but it may. And military conflict could be difficult. An Iraqi regime faced with its own demise may attempt cruel and desperate measures. If Saddam Hussein orders such measures, his generals would be well advised to refuse those orders. If they do not refuse, they must understand that all war criminals will be pursued and punished. If we have to act, we will take every precaution that is possible. We will plan carefully, we will act with the full power of the United States military, we will act with allies at our side, and we will prevail. (Applause.)

There is no easy or risk-free course of action. Some have argued we should wait—and that's an option. In my view, it's the riskiest of all options, because the longer we wait, the stronger and bolder Saddam Hussein will become. We could wait and hope that Saddam does not give weapons to terrorists, or develop a nuclear weapon to blackmail the world. But I'm convinced that is a hope against all evidence. As Americans, we want peace—we work and sacrifice for peace. But there can be no peace if our security depends on the will and whims of a ruthless and aggressive dictator. I'm not willing to stake one American life on trusting Saddam Hussein.

Failure to act would embolden other tyrants, allow terrorists access to new weapons and new resources, and make blackmail a permanent feature of world events. The United Nations would betray the purpose of its founding, and prove irrelevant to the problems of our time. And through its inaction, the United States would resign itself to a future of fear.

That is not the America I know. That is not the America I serve. We refuse to live in fear. (Applause.) This nation, in world war and in Cold War, has never permitted the brutal and lawless to set history's course. Now, as before, we will secure our nation, protect our freedom, and help others to find freedom of their own.

Some worry that a change of leadership in Iraq could create instability and make the situation worse. The situation could hardly get worse, for world security and for the people of Iraq. The lives of Iraqi citizens would improve dramatically if Saddam Hussein were no longer in power, just as the lives of Afghanistan's citizens improved after the Taliban. The dictator of Iraq is a student of Stalin, using murder as a tool of terror and control, within his own cabinet, within his own army, and even within his own family.

On Saddam Hussein's orders, opponents have been decapitated, wives and mothers of political opponents have been systematically raped as a method of intimidation, and political prisoners have been forced to watch their own children being tortured.

America believes that all people are entitled to hope and human rights, to the non-negotiable demands of human dignity. People everywhere prefer freedom to slavery, prosperity to squalor, self-government to the rule of terror and torture. America is a friend to the people of Iraq. Our demands are directed only at the regime that enslaves them and threatens us. When these demands are met, the first and greatest benefit will come to Iraqi men, women, and children. The oppression of Kurds, Assyrians, Turkomans, Shi'a, Sunnis, and others will be lifted. The long captivity of Iraq will end, and an era of new hope will begin.

Iraq is a land rich in culture, resources, and talent. Freed from the weight of oppression, Iraq's people will be able to share in the progress and prosperity of our time. If military action is necessary, the United States and our allies will help the Iraqi people rebuild their economy and create the institutions of liberty in a unified Iraq at peace with its neighbors.

Later this week, the United States Congress will vote on this matter. I have asked Congress to authorize the use of America's military, if it proves necessary, to enforce UN Security Council demands. Approving this resolution does not mean that military action is imminent or unavoidable. The resolution will tell the United Nations, and all nations, that America speaks with one voice and is determined to make the demands of the civilized world mean something. Congress will also be sending a message to the dictator in Iraq: that his only chance—his only choice—is full compliance, and the time remaining for that choice is limited.

Members of Congress are nearing an historic vote. I'm confident they will fully consider the facts, and their duties.

The attacks of September the 11th showed our country that vast oceans no longer protect us from danger. Before that tragic date, we had only hints of Al Qaeda's plans and designs. Today in Iraq, we see a threat whose outlines are far more clearly defined, and whose consequences could be far more deadly. Saddam Hussein's actions have put us on notice, and there is no refuge from our responsibilities.

We did not ask for this present challenge, but we accept it. Like other generations of Americans, we will meet the responsibility of defending human liberty against violence and aggression. By our resolve, we will give strength to others. By our courage, we will give hope to others. And by our actions, we will secure the peace, and lead the world to a better day.

May God bless America. (Applause.)

Terrorism Grows in the Absence of Progress[5]

Condoleezza Rice

Assistant to the president of the United States for National Security Affairs, 2001– ; born Birmingham, AL, November 14, 1954; bachelor's degree cum laude and Phi Beta Kappa, University of Denver, 1974; master's degree in political science, University of Notre Dame, 1975; Ph.D. in political science, University of Denver's Graduate School of International Studies, 1981; fellow in the arms control and disarmament program, Stanford University, 1981; assistant, associate, then full professor of political science, Stanford University, 1981–99; national fellow, Hoover Institution, 1985–86; international affairs fellow of the Council on Foreign Relations and special assistant to the director of the Joint Chiefs of Staff, 1986; director and senior director of Soviet and East European Affairs in the National Security Council, 1989–91; senior fellow, Hoover Institution, 1991–93; provost, Stanford University, 1993–99; National Endowment for the Humanities trustee; fellow of the American Academy of Arts and Sciences; honorary degrees from Morehouse College, 1991, University of Alabama, 1994, and University of Notre Dame, 1995; has written numerous articles and several books on international relations and foreign affairs, including Germany Unified and Europe Transformed: A Study in Statecraft *(1995).*

Editors' introduction: On May 1, 2003, after roughly six weeks of war against President Saddam Hussein's regime in Iraq, President Bush announced an end to combat operations and declared, "The United States and our allies have prevailed." National Security Adviser Rice told 1,500 persons attending the Town Hall Los Angeles Breakfast that, "In Iraq, a murderous tyrant and a supporter of terror has been defeated, and a free society is rising," then cautioned, "The transition from dictatorship to democracy will take time, but it is worth every effort." Town Hall Los Angeles is a nonprofit, nonpartisan civic forum that presents speakers across the spectrum of opinion.

Condoleezza Rice's speech: Well, thank you very much for that warm welcome. It's so great to be here at the Town Hall, Los Angeles. I want to thank Liam McGee for that terrific introduction and for his work as vice chair of Town Hall Los Angeles. Adrienne

---

5. Delivered on June 12, 2003, at Los Angeles, CA.

Medawar, the president of Town Hall Los Angeles, thank you for
your hard work. And to all of the board members and staff members who make this great organization function, thank you very
much.

I see a lot of familiar faces here—friends from the academy, a
family member, a number of longtime friends from California. It's
just great to be home—thank you very much for welcoming me
here.

My time at Stanford—as professor and provost—provided some
of the fondest memories of my career. And, like Stanford, Town
Hall Los Angeles thrives on debate and discussion about the great
issues of the day. I want to spend a few minutes speaking with you
today about an issue that is clearly vital to our time—promoting
peace and progress and change in the Middle East.

The events of the last few months make clear that the
Middle East is living through a time of great change.
And despite the tragic events of the past few days, it is
also a time of great hope. President Bush believes that
the region is at a true turning point. He believes that
the people of the Middle East have a real chance to
build a future of peace and freedom and opportunity.

In Iraq, a murderous tyrant and a supporter of terror
has been defeated, and a free society is rising. Coalition
troops in Iraq still face great dangers each and every
day. Iraq's transition from dictatorship to democracy is
proving every bit as challenging as we had imagined.
Three decades of tyranny left Iraq worse off than we
had imagined.

In Iraq, a murderous tyrant and a supporter of terror has been defeated, and a free society is rising.

Saddam's palaces were in very good repair. And years
of intelligence and UN reports tell us that his weapons
of mass destruction programs were robust and well-funded. But
Iraq's water and sewer systems and power grids and hospitals and
schools all suffer from decades of malign neglect. The psychological
impact of decades of murderous totalitarianism on generations of
Iraqis is even worse. Truth was buried with thousands of Iraqis in
mass graves that are still being discovered. Trust was imprisoned
with children jailed on the capricious whims of a brutal regime.

We are working with the Iraqi people to stabilize their country, to
improve security and to make basic services better than they were
before the war. But much hard work remains. America and our
coalition partners are determined to do the work that we came to
do, and then we will leave.

President Bush has stated many times that the battle of Iraq was
about moving a great danger, but also about building a better
future for all of the people of the region. Iraq's people, for sure, will
be the first to benefit. But success in Iraq will also add to the
momentum for reform that is already touching lives, from Morocco
to Bahrain and beyond.

Last year, in an extraordinary United Nations report, leading Arab intellectuals called for greater political and economic freedom for the empowerment of women, and better and more modern education in the Arab world. In January of this year, Crown Prince Abdullah of Saudi Arabia proposed an Arab Charter to spur economic and political reform. And the proposal speaks openly of the need for enhanced political participation. In Afghanistan, people are rebuilding, writing a new constitution and moving beyond the culture of the warlord that has dominated their political life for a generation.

> *Reform takes time, and it is often difficult. There is no one-size-fits-all model of democracy.*

The world has a vital interest in seeing these efforts succeed, and a responsibility to help. As President Bush said, stable and free nations do not breed the ideologies of murder, they encourage the peaceful pursuit of a better life. Of course, reform takes time, and it is often difficult. There is no one-size-fits-all model of democracy. New liberties can find an honored place among treasured traditions.

Everyone must reject, nonetheless, the condescending view that freedom will not grow in the soil of the Middle East, or that Muslims somehow do not share the desire to be free. The United States has made clear that we stand with all people in the Muslim world and around the globe who seek creative freedom, greater opportunity.

The president has a comprehensive strategy for the Middle East. He has proposed the creation of a U.S.–Middle East free trade area within a decade, so that people of the region can tap the power of global markets to build their own prosperity. And the president has put the United States firmly behind the creation of a state called Palestine, that is viable, peaceful, and free.

Peace between Israelis and Palestinians will not result from the will of a single leader. But as the president said last week, achieving peace in the Middle East is a matter of the highest priority for the United States. We can help the parties, and we will help the parties. But the hardest work must be done by the parties, themselves.

The pictures you saw and the words you heard last week from the Red Sea were historic. I'd like to take a moment to look at the groundwork that led to those extraordinary moments.

Almost a year ago, in his speech on June 24th of 2002, the president laid out a vision for a new Middle East. That vision was clear: two states, Israel and Palestine, living side-by-side in peace and security. The means to realize that vision were also clear—and, in fact, a little controversial.

First, and famously, the president called on the Palestinians to bring about new leaders, leaders not compromised by terror. The old leadership had failed to deliver on the promises to fight terror, but had, in fact, encouraged it and even abetted it. As a result, President Bush believed that new leadership was needed. And because of his faith in the hopes and aspirations of the Palestinian people, he believed it was possible.

We all had to be patient. But the Palestinians have begun to take their own future into their hands. And they understand the new leadership, that there can be no peace for either side until there is freedom for both sides.

> *The Palestinian people deserve the same things that many of us take for granted every day.*

The Palestinian people deserve the same things that many of us take for granted every day: the rule of law, economic freedom, and democratic institutions, the right to live in dignity. A reformed, democratic Palestine would not only meet the aspirations of the Palestinian people, its first and most important task, but it would also inspire confidence by Israel that a true partner for peace had emerged in the Gaza and the West Bank.

The president, in that same speech, stressed that there was a need for all sides to meet their responsibilities—not just Palestinians, but Israelis and Arab states, too. The Israelis must deal with settlement activity, dismantle outposts, and ease the daily humiliation faced by ordinary Palestinians. The Palestinians must fight terror and end incitement.

But real progress requires all of us to recognize that there are more than just two parties with responsibilities in this conflict. The Arab states, the neighboring states must be partners in that peace. They have influence with the Palestinians and they must use it to encourage reform and promote peace. They, too, have responsibilities to fight terror and incitement among their own people.

In the 50 weeks since that June 24th speech, the United States has held fast to that vision. The president has sought to bring life to it through engagement with the parties when engagement would help. During that time, he spoke to and met with leaders and all sides. He instructed Secretary Powell to work closely with his counterparts from the United Nations, Russia, and the European Union to put together a concrete plan for realizing the vision of two states—a plan that came to be known as the road map.

At the same time, Arab states were showing a new willingness to support reform both at home and in Palestinian territories. And, of course, new Palestinian leadership did begin to emerge. Mahmoud Abbas—a man committed to fighting terror, who has described the intifada that began in 2000 as a mistake—became prime minister. He appointed, in turn, a reformist cabinet that included a finance minister, the respected Salaam Fayyad, who is already pursuing the discipline and transparency necessary to put Palestinian finances in order and to assure that Palestinian resources benefit the people and not the terrorists. And the Israeli government formally endorsed the idea of a Palestinian state located along its borders.

In short, the strategic landscape of the region is vastly different than it was just a little less than a year ago. And this is the backdrop to the pictures and the words that came from the Red Sea last week.

In Sharm el-Sheikh, the Arab leaders rejected terror in the strongest possible terms. They vowed to fight the scourge of terrorism and reject the culture of extremism and violence in any form or shape for whatever source or place, regardless of justification or motivation. They vowed to use all the power of the law to prevent support reaching terrorist groups. And they committed themselves to helping the Palestinian Authority fight terror and to helping Palestinians and Israelis build representative democratic institutions in their own territories. They also committed to a democratic Iraq that would build representative and stable institutions.

This is a time for all who are committed to peace to speak and act against the enemies of peace.

As Arab governments put these pledges into place it put a premium now on action. Because words can greatly aid the momentum toward peace, but only if there is action.

In Aqaba, Prime Ministers Sharon and Abbas declared their commitment to a peace founded on the vision of two states. And they committed to taking tangible steps to bring that peace closer.

Prime Minister Sharon pledged to improve the humanitarian situation in the Palestinian areas and to begin removing unauthorized outposts immediately. He recognized the importance of territorial contiguity for a viable Palestinian state. And he said: It is in Israel's interest not to govern Palestinians, but for the Palestinians to govern themselves in their own state.

Prime Minister Abbas recognized that terrorism is not a means to a Palestinian state, but a deadly obstacle to it. He pledged to use his full efforts to end the armed intifada and to work without compromise for the end of violence and terror. He also pledged to make Palestinian institutions, including security services, more democratic and accountable.

Of course, the hopeful picture I've outlined is just a beginning. This week has seen familiar scenes of bloodshed and violence caused by those who would use terror to destroy the hopes of the many for peace. The terrorists will not succeed. This is a time for all who are committed to peace to speak and act against the enemies of peace. President Bush remains committed to the course set at Aqaba because it is the only course that will bring a durable peace and lasting security.

This president keeps his promises. He expects all the parties to keep theirs.

More than four decades ago, President Kennedy spoke of a long twilight schedule, year in and year out, against the common enemies of man: tyranny, poverty, disease, and war, itself.

Some champions of these evils have been vanquished, but the common enemies of man remain, and a new enemy—global terror—has emerged. The United States is determined to fight this new enemy, knowing full well that final victory will probably not come any time soon.

On September 20th, shortly after the September 11th attacks, the president told the American people that that victory might, in fact, might not even come on his watch. This enemy is different from any we have ever known. Stateless, stealthy, small terror networks can wreak untold damage without warning anywhere in the world. Their strategy is to use wanton destruction and the slaughter of innocents to sow confusion and to hold human progress as a heresy. They have no territory or assets. They cannot be deterred. They have no interests beyond the killing of innocents. They can not be persuaded. They can only be destroyed.

But the fever swamps in which they grow can be drained. The emergence of new networks and new recruits can be prevented. The war on terror is as much a war of ideas as a war of force. To win the broader war, we must win this war of ideas by appealing to the just aspirations and decent hopes of people throughout the world—giving them cause to hope for a better life and a brighter future, and reason to reject the false and destructive comforts of bitterness and grievance and hate.

Terror grows in the absence of progress and development. It thrives in the airless space where new ideas, new hopes, and new aspirations are forbidden. Terror lives where freedom dies.

That is why fighting the common enemies of man is not only the right thing to do, it is the clear, vital interest of the world to do so.

In the defeat of communism and all through the post–World War II transformation of Europe and Asia, America and her allies demonstrated that we can and do stay the course until the work is done. The defeat of global terror and the emergence of a freer, more prosperous and more modern Middle East may also be the work of a generation.

At this time of hope and promise, we and those who share our values must work together to create a world where terror is shunned and hope is the provenance of every living human.

The long twilight struggle continues. Thank you very much for having me here.

The Road to Cover-up Is the Road to Ruin[6]

Robert C. Byrd

U.S. senator from West Virginia, 1959– ; born North Wilkesboro, NC, November 20, 1917; high school in West Virginia, 1930s; welder during World War II building Liberty *and* Victory *ships in Baltimore, MD, and Tampa, FL; West Virginia House of Representatives, 1947–50; West Virginia Senate, 1951–52; B.A. in political science summa cum laude, Marshall University, 1952; Senate Appropriations Committee, 1959– ; J.D. cum laude, American University Law School, 1963; Senate Democratic whip, 1971; Senate majority leader, 1977–80, 1987–88; Senate minority leader, 1981–86; chairman, Senate Appropriations Committee, 2001; authored four volumes of U.S. Senate speeches and* The Senate of the Roman Republic: Addresses on the History of Roman Constitutionalism *(1995); Mason (33rd degree).*

Editors' introduction: One justification President Bush gave for sending troops to Iraq was the perceived threat to the United States and the world posed by Iraq's weapons of "mass destruction." After the president announced the official end of "combat operations" in Iraq on May 1, 2003, the search for those weapons increased. When no such weapons were found, critics of the war argued that the official intelligence upon which the Bush administration based its claim of the existence of biological and chemical weapons was inaccurate. Senator Byrd questioned the reliability of the "hand-picked intelligence" used by the administration and insisted, "The American people have questions that need to be answered about why we went to war with Iraq."

Robert C. Byrd's speech: Mr. President, last fall, the White House released a national security strategy that called for an end to the doctrines of deterrence and containment that have been a hallmark of American foreign policy for more than half a century.

This new national security strategy is based upon preemptive war against those who might threaten our security.

Such a strategy of striking first against possible dangers is heavily reliant upon interpretation of accurate and timely intelligence. If we are going to hit first, based on perceived dangers, the perceptions had better be accurate. If our intelligence is faulty, we may launch

---

6. Delivered on June 24, 2003, on the floor of the U.S. Senate, Washington, D.C.

preemptive wars against countries that do not pose a real threat against us. Or we may overlook countries that do pose real threats to our security, allowing us no chance to pursue diplomatic solutions to stop a crisis before it escalates to war. In either case lives could be needlessly lost. In other words, we had better be certain that we can discern the imminent threats from the false alarms.

Ninety-six days ago [as of June 24], President Bush announced that he had initiated a war to "disarm Iraq, to free its people, and to defend the world from grave danger." The president told the world: "Our nation enters this conflict reluctantly—yet, our purpose is sure. The people of the United States and our friends and allies will not live at the mercy of an outlaw regime that threatens the peace with weapons of mass murder." [Address to the Nation, 3/19/03]

The president has since announced that major combat operations concluded on May 1. He said: "Major combat operations in Iraq have ended. In the battle of Iraq, the United States and our allies have prevailed." Since then, the United States has been recognized by the international community as the occupying power in Iraq. And yet, we have not found any evidence that would confirm the officially stated reason that our country was sent to war: namely, that Iraq's weapons of mass destruction constituted a grave threat to the United States.

We have not found any evidence that would confirm the officially stated reason that our country was sent to war.

We have heard a lot about revisionist history from the White House of late in answer to those who question whether there was a real threat from Iraq. But, it is the president who appears to me to be intent on revising history. There is an abundance of clear and unmistakable evidence that the administration sought to portray Iraq as a direct and deadly threat to the American people. But there is a great difference between the hand-picked intelligence that was presented by the administration to Congress and the American people when compared against what we have actually discovered in Iraq. This Congress and the people who sent us here are entitled to an explanation from the administration.

On January 28, 2003, President Bush said in his State of the Union Address: "The British government has learned that Saddam Hussein recently sought significant quantities of uranium from Africa." [State of the Union, 1/28/03] Yet, according to news reports, the CIA knew that this claim was false as early as March 2002. In addition, the International Atomic Energy Agency has since discredited this allegation.

On February 5, Secretary of State Colin Powell told the United Nations Security Council: "Our conservative estimate is that Iraq today has a stockpile of between 100 and 500 tons of chemical weapons agent. That is enough to fill 16,000 battlefield rockets."

[Remarks to UN Security Council, 2/5/03] The truth is, to date we have not found any of this material, nor those thousands of rockets loaded with chemical weapons.

On February 8, President Bush told the nation: "We have sources that tell us that Saddam Hussein recently authorized Iraqi field commanders to use chemical weapons—the very weapons the dictator tells us he does not have." [Radio Address, 2/8/03] Mr. President, we are all relieved that such weapons were not used, but it has not yet been explained why the Iraqi army did not use them. Did the Iraqi army flee their positions before chemical weapons could be used? If so, why were the weapons not left behind? Or is it that the army was never issued chemical weapons? We need answers.

On March 16, the Sunday before the war began, in an interview with Tim Russert, Vice President Cheney said that Iraqis want "to get rid of Saddam Hussein, and they will welcome as liberators the United States when we come to do that." He added, "the vast majority of them would turn [Saddam Hussein] in in a minute if, in fact, they thought they could do so safely." [*Meet the Press*, 3/16/03] But in fact, Mr. President, today Iraqi cities remain in disorder, our troops are under attack, our occupation government lives and works in fortified compounds, and we are still trying to determine the fate of the ousted, murderous dictator.

The Administration's rhetoric played upon the well-founded fear of the American public about future acts of terrorism.

On March 30, Secretary of Defense Donald Rumsfeld, during the height of the war, said of the search for weapons of mass destruction: "We know where they are. They're in the area around Tikrit and Baghdad and east, west, south, and north somewhat." [*This Week*, 3/30/03] But Baghdad fell to our troops on April 9, and Tikrit on April 14, and the intelligence Secretary Rumsfeld spoke about has not led us to any weapons of mass destruction.

Whether or not intelligence reports were bent, stretched, or massaged to make Iraq look like an imminent threat to the United States, it is clear that the administration's rhetoric played upon the well-founded fear of the American public about future acts of terrorism. But, upon close examination, many of these statements have nothing to do with intelligence, because they are at root just sound bites based on conjecture. They are designed to prey on public fear.

The face of Osama bin Laden morphed into that of Saddam Hussein. President Bush carefully blurred these images in his State of the Union Address. Listen to this quote from his State of the Union Address: "Imagine those 19 hijackers with other weapons and other plans—this time armed by Saddam Hussein. It would take one vial, one canister, one crate slipped into this country to bring a day of horror like none we have ever known." [State of the Union, 1/28/03] Judging by this speech, not only is the president confusing Al Qaeda and Iraq, but he also appears to give a vote of no-confidence to our homeland security efforts. Isn't the White House the brains behind the Department of Homeland Security? Isn't the administration supposed to be stopping those vials, canisters, and crates from entering our country, rather than trying to scare our fellow citizens half to death about them?

Not only did the administration warn about more hijackers carrying deadly chemicals, the White House even went so far as to suggest that the time it would take for UN inspectors to find solid, "smoking gun" evidence of Saddam's illegal weapons would put the U.S. at greater risk of a nuclear attack from Iraq. National Security Adviser Condoleezza Rice was quoted as saying on September 9, 2002, by the *Los Angeles Times*, "We don't want the 'smoking gun' to be a mushroom cloud." [*Los Angeles Times*, "Threat by Iraq Grows, U.S. Says," 9/9/02] Talk about hype! Mushroom clouds? Where is the evidence for this? There isn't any.

On September 26, 2002, just two weeks before Congress voted on a resolution to allow the president to invade Iraq, and six weeks before the midterm elections, President Bush himself built the case that Iraq was plotting to attack the United States. After meeting with members of Congress on that date, the president said: "The danger to our country is grave. The danger to our country is growing. The Iraqi regime possesses biological and chemical weapons. . . . The regime is seeking a nuclear bomb, and with fissile material, could build one within a year."

These are the president's words. He said that Saddam Hussein is "seeking a nuclear bomb." Have we found any evidence to date of this chilling allegation? No.

But, President Bush continued on that autumn day: "The dangers we face will only worsen from month to month and from year to year. To ignore these threats is to encourage them. And when they have fully materialized it may be too late to protect ourselves and our friends and our allies. By then the Iraqi dictator would have the means to terrorize and dominate the region. Each passing day could be the one on which the Iraqi regime gives anthrax or VX—nerve gas—or some day a nuclear weapon to a terrorist ally." [Rose Garden Remarks, 9/26/02]

And yet, seven weeks after declaring victory in the war against Iraq, we have seen nary a shred of evidence to support his claims of grave dangers, chemical weapons, links to Al Qaeda, or nuclear weapons.

Just days before a vote on a resolution that handed the president unprecedented war powers, President Bush stepped up the scare tactics. On October 7, just four days before the October 11 vote in the Senate on the war resolution, the president stated: "We know that Iraq and the Al Qaeda terrorist network share a common enemy—the United States of America. We know that Iraq and Al Qaeda have had high-level contacts that go back a decade." President Bush continued: "We've learned that Iraq has trained Al

Qaeda members in bomb-making and poisons and deadly gases. . . . Alliance with terrorists could allow the Iraqi regime to attack America without leaving any fingerprints."

President Bush also elaborated on claims of Iraq's nuclear program when he said: "The evidence indicates that Iraq is reconstituting its nuclear weapons program. Saddam Hussein has held numerous meetings with Iraqi nuclear scientists, a group he calls his 'nuclear mujahideen'—his nuclear holy warriors. . . . If the Iraqi regime is able to produce, buy, or steal an amount of highly enriched uranium a little larger than a single softball, it could have a nuclear weapon in less than a year." [Cincinnati Museum Center, 10/7/02]

This is the kind of pumped up intelligence and outrageous rhetoric that were given to the American people to justify war with Iraq. This is the same kind of hyped evidence that was given to Congress to sway its vote for war on October 11, 2002.

We hear some voices say, but why should we care? After all, the United States won the war, didn't it? Saddam Hussein is no more; he is either dead or on the run. What does it matter if reality does not reveal the same grim picture that was so carefully painted before the war? So what if the menacing characterizations that conjured up visions of mushroom clouds and American cities threatened with deadly germs and chemicals were overdone? So what?

Mr. President, our sons and daughters who serve in uniform answered a call to duty. They were sent to the hot sands of the Middle East to fight in a war that has already cost the lives of 194 Americans, thousands of innocent civilians, and unknown numbers of Iraqi soldiers. Our troops are still at risk. Hardly a day goes by that there is not another attack on the troops who are trying to restore order to a country teetering on the brink of anarchy. When are they coming home?

The president told the American people that we were compelled to go to war to secure our country from a grave threat. Are we any safer today than we were on March 18, 2003? Our nation has been committed to rebuilding a country ravaged by war and tyranny, and the cost of that task is being paid in blood and treasure every day.

It is in the compelling national interest to examine what we were told about the threat from Iraq. It is in the compelling national interest to know if the intelligence was faulty. It is in the compelling national interest to know if the intelligence was distorted.

Mr. President, Congress must face this issue squarely. Congress should begin immediately an investigation into the intelligence that was presented to the American people about the pre-war estimates of Saddam's weapons of mass destruction and the way in which that intelligence might have been misused. This is no time for a timid Congress. We have a responsibility to act in the national interest and protect the American people. We must get to the bottom of this matter.

Although some timorous steps have been taken in the past few days to begin a review of this intelligence—I must watch my terms carefully, for I may be tempted to use the words "investigation" or "inquiry" to describe this review, and those are terms which I am told are not supposed to be used—the proposed measures appear to fall short of what the situation requires. We are already shading our terms about how to describe the proposed review of intelligence: cherry-picking words to give the American people the impression that the government is fully in control of the situation, and that there is no reason to ask tough questions. This is the same problem that got us into this controversy about slanted intelligence reports. Word games. Lots and lots of word games.

Well, Mr. President, this is no game. For the first time in our history, the United States has gone to war because of intelligence reports claiming that a country posed a threat to our nation. Congress should not be content to use standard operating procedures to look into this extraordinary matter. We should accept no substitute for a full, bipartisan investigation by Congress into the issue of our pre-war intelligence on the threat from Iraq and its use.

The purpose of such an investigation is not to play pre-election year politics, nor is it to engage in what some might call "revisionist history." Rather it is to get at the truth. The longer questions are allowed to fester about what our intelligence knew about Iraq, and when they knew it, the greater the risk that the people—the American people whom we are elected to serve—will lose confidence in our government.

This looming crisis of trust is not limited to the public. Many of my colleagues were willing to trust the administration and vote to authorize war against Iraq. Many members of this body trusted so much that they gave the president sweeping authority to commence war. As President Reagan famously said, "Trust, but verify." Despite my opposition, the Senate voted to blindly trust the president with unprecedented power to declare war. While the reconstruction continues, so do the questions, and it is time to verify.

I have served the people of West Virginia in Congress for half a century. I have witnessed deceit and scandal, cover-up and aftermath. I have seen presidents of both parties who once enjoyed great popularity among the people leave office in disgrace because they misled the American people. I say to this administration: Do not circle the wagons. Do not discourage the seeking of truth in these matters.

Mr. President, the American people have questions that need to be answered about why we went to war with Iraq. To attempt to deny the relevance of these questions is to trivialize the people's trust.

The business of intelligence is secretive by necessity, but our government is open by design. We must be straight with the American people. Congress has the obligation to investigate the use of intelligence information by the administration, in the open, so that the American people can see that those who exercise power, especially the awesome power of preemptive war, must be held accountable. We must not go down the road of cover-up. That is the road to ruin.

II. Homeland Security

Senate Appropriations Committee[1]

Norman Y. Mineta

Secretary of Transportation, 2001– ; born San Jose, CA, November 12, 1931; B.S., University of California, Berkeley, 1953; intelligence officer, U.S. Army, 1954–56; joined his father in the Mineta Insurance Agency before serving as first Asian Pacific American member of City Council of San Jose, CA, 1967–71; mayor of San Jose (first Asian Pacific American to serve as mayor of a major U.S. city), 1971–74; U.S. House of Representatives, 1975–95, and chairman of the House's Committee on Public Works and Transportation, 1992–94; vice president, special business initiatives, Lockheed Martin Corporation, 1995–2000; U.S. secretary of Commerce (first Asian Pacific American to serve in a presidential cabinet), 2000; chairman, National Civic Aviation Review Commission, 1997; with his family, among the 120,000 Japanese Americans forced into internment camps during World War II; in Congress, driving force behind passage of H.R. 442, the Civil Liberties Act of 1988, officially apologizing for and redressing the injustices done to Japanese Americans during World War II; Martin Luther King, Jr., Commemorative Medal for contributions to the field of civil rights, George Washington University, 1995.

Editors' introduction: On September 11, 2001, terrorists hijacked airplanes over United States soil and killed thousands of Americans and citizens from some 80 other countries in New York, Washington, D.C., and Pennsylvania. Nearly a month later President Bush established the White House Office of Homeland Security. On January 24, 2003, the president elevated that office to cabinet status, introducing Tom Ridge as the secretary of the newly created Department of Homeland Security. Concerned about protecting the nation's air- and waterways, Secretary Mineta outlined for the U.S. Senate Appropriations Committee what steps the government was taking to "provide all Americans with a safe, reliable, efficient, and secure transportation system."

Norman Y. Mineta's testimony: Good morning Mr. Chairman, Senator Stevens, and members of the committee. I am pleased to have the opportunity to appear before you today to discuss the ongoing work of the Department of Transportation (DOT) in addressing our nation's homeland security challenges. The events of September 11th underscore the importance of transportation

---

1. Delivered on May 2, 2002, at Washington, D.C.

security as a major part of America's homeland security. Protecting airports, seaports, railroads, bridges, highways, and mass transportation facilities against the threat of terrorism is imperative. The terrorist attacks have resulted in a renewed focus on the security of our transportation systems and we at DOT are moving forward aggressively to meet these challenges on several fronts.

Today, I would like to share with you some of the initiatives under way at the department that I believe demonstrate our commitment to improving homeland security for all Americans and to ask for your support in providing the resources we need to get the job done as quickly and efficiently as possible.

Protecting Our Nation's Airways

Let me begin by thanking the Congress for its support and encouragement as we continue to establish the new Transportation Security Administration (TSA). The department is working diligently to meet the deadlines established in the Aviation and Transportation Security Act, and I am proud of the work achieved to date. This new agency has met each of its deadlines and is on the path to continued success.

Protecting airports, seaports, railroads, bridges, highways, and mass transportation facilities against the threat of terrorism is imperative.

TSA successfully established a system for screening all checked baggage by the January 18th deadline. It required continuous use of bulk explosive detection systems (EDS) to screen checked bags at those airports where EDS are located and ensured the use of positive passenger bag match for checked baggage screening at those airports where EDS is currently unavailable. TSA has provided other security improvements as well, including greater use of trace explosive detection systems (ETD) on checked baggage, more use of explosive detection canine teams, and physical inspection of checked bags.

TSA developed a plan for training federal screeners, which was written with input from leading government and private sector training experts. It also issued interim final rules to implement the $2.50 September 11th Passenger Security Fee on airline tickets sold on or after February 1st, as well as the Aviation Security Infrastructure Fee that will be paid by air carriers to help finance TSA operations. In addition, U.S. and foreign air carriers now electronically transmit passenger and crew manifests to the U.S. Customs Service prior to arrival, and the Federal Aviation Administration (FAA) issued its guidelines for flight crews who face threats onboard an aircraft.

On February 17, the undersecretary of transportation for security took over all civil aviation security functions performed by the FAA. On that date, the TSA also assumed airline-screening company contracts in the interim until federal security screeners can be hired, trained, and assigned to all U.S. airport security screening checkpoints. TSA also published a rule requiring certain aircraft operators using aircraft weighing 12,500 pounds or more to implement a security program that includes criminal history records checks on their flight crews and restricted access to the flight deck. These security regulations apply to both all-cargo and small scheduled and charter passenger aircraft not already covered by a security program and will take effect on June 24, 2002.

Additional key components of securing our airports will be a combination of technology and alternative inspection methods. The use of explosive detection equipment is a vital part of our enhanced baggage-screening program. TSA is committed to ensuring that every available explosive detection system and device will be continuously used.

We are confronted with numerous initiatives over the next several weeks and months and need your support to be successful in meeting these challenges. We must federalize the screening contracts; hire and train passenger screeners to meet the November 19, 2002, deadline; hire and train baggage screeners to meet the December 31, 2002, deadline; recruit and train federal security directors at 429 airports; and hire and train a mix of federal and state law enforcement officers to support our efforts at all local airports.

These new initiatives are among many the TSA is using to achieve its aviation security goals. I would now like to discuss some specific security initiatives involving TSA and other parts of DOT.

Protecting Our Nation's Waterways and Maritime Borders

Although aviation security has to date been the major emphasis at TSA, we must also remain focused on the threats to our homeland from vulnerabilities in other transportation systems as well. TSA is working closely with the other operating administrations within DOT—the United States Coast Guard, the Maritime Administration, and the Saint Lawrence Seaway Development Corporation—to address potential vulnerabilities in our nation's ports and waterways.

Every day thousands of containers enter our U.S. ports and waterways from abroad, providing another possible avenue for a terrorist threat. Since September 11th the department has taken a number of critical steps to improve port security:

- The Coast Guard has enhanced its presence to protect critical bridges, port facilities, and other infrastructure.

- The Coast Guard, in collaboration with the U.S. Customs Service, has issued an emergency regulation requiring 96-hour advance notice of arrival for ships entering U.S. ports, and is taking steps to make this a standard operating procedure by the summer of 2002.

- The Coast Guard Intelligence Coordination Center, working with the Office of Naval Intelligence, has been tracking high-interest vessels entering our ports and is providing intelligence on the people, cargoes, and vessels to operational commanders and interested agencies.

- The Coast Guard has deployed sea marshals and small boat escorts to accompany vessels containing critical cargoes and those traveling through sensitive areas. The Coast Guard is assessing ports to make federal, state, and local government agencies and other appropriate stakeholders aware of the susceptibility of all facets of maritime critical infrastructure.

- The Maritime Administration is working jointly with U.S. Customs, exporters and importers, carriers and governments to establish business and security practices that will push the nation's virtual borders outward to the point of loading of containers.

- The Coast Guard has engaged the International Maritime Organization (IMO) in the development of international maritime security procedures that we hope will be adopted by the IMO later this year.

- The Maritime Administration, Research and Special Programs Administration, and TSA are working to examine ways that advanced technologies, including "smart cards" and biometrics, can be used throughout the maritime and related industries in order to accurately identify employees working in security-sensitive areas.

- The Research and Special Programs Administration is leading an effort within DOT to identify innovative concepts or new applications of proven technology, methods, or processes for improving security of containers throughout global transportation supply chains.

- The St. Lawrence Seaway Development Corporation has been working closely with its Canadian counterpart and the Coast Guard to heighten security on the St. Lawrence River and ensure the protection of ocean access to our Great Lakes ports.

These initiatives illustrate some of the many ongoing activities under way at the department to address security concerns affecting our ports and waterways. Also, we are actively working with the Senate and the House on enactment of port security legislation in this Congress.

Improving Border Security

In the aftermath of the September 11th attacks, we know we cannot have border security without effective transportation security. But President Bush and I believe that America can and must accommodate both reliable security and economic growth. Within the last four months this administration has signed "smart border" accords with both Canada and Mexico precisely to develop joint action plans to ensure the secure and efficient flow of people and goods across not only our borders, but across trade corridors that stretch from northern Canada to southern Mexico and beyond. Transportation security and effective border management are different sides of the same coin. As the lead federal department for Intelligent Transportation Systems, and overseeing the transportation systems that move both people and goods, I am proud of the department's role in supporting innovative projects that pull together key federal and state agencies for transportation safety, security, and efficiency.

Transportation security and effective border management are different sides of the same coin.

Protecting Surface Transportation Facilities

Surface transportation security must also be a priority focus for our department. Every American depends on our nation's highways and mass transit and rail systems to get us where we need to go. The Federal Highway Administration (FHWA) has increased efforts to heighten security and surveillance of critical highway infrastructure including vital connectors to our ports, railroads, and military bases. FHWA is working with state departments of transportation and local transportation officials to conduct vulnerability assessments and to establish protection strategies. Furthermore, the Federal Motor Carrier Safety Administration is working to ensure that trucks crossing the borders into the United States have been properly inspected and meet security and safety requirements.

The Federal Transit Administration (FTA) is assessing the security of high-risk transit assets including vulnerabilities in subway tunnels and stations where large numbers of people converge and where an attack would cause the greatest disruption to transportation services. FTA is working with local systems to develop best practices to improve communication systems and develop emergency response plans.

Similarly, the Federal Railroad Administration (FRA) is assisting the rail industry in conducting security assessments of our freight rail system. The security of hazardous materials including radioactive materials and defense-related shipments are two areas that have received special emphasis. FRA is also assisting Amtrak in enhancing the security and safety of New York City tunnels under the East and Hudson Rivers. FRA is currently developing with Amtrak a grant agreement specifying the projects that will utilize the $100 million in emergency supplemental funds provided to Amtrak for improving the security of these tunnels. Funds are anticipated to be obligated shortly.

Another area of concern with respect to public safety is the security of our nation's pipeline systems. To keep our pipelines secure to the maximum extent possible, we have streamlined the communication process with our federal, state and industry partners, to ensure security information and threat warnings are available on a real-time basis. The Research and Special Programs Administration continues to focus on implementing a coordinated set of protocols for our inspectors to use to verify that operators are putting security practices into place at critical facilities.

Coordination Both Within DOT and Among Other Agencies

A key element in our continued success to address our homeland security objectives requires improvements in communication and coordination among DOT operating administrations, and other federal agencies.

To address some of the need for improved communication, last fall I established the National Infrastructure Security Committee (NISC), a coordinated effort to address transportation security. Through several direct action groups, the NISC has evaluated transportation infrastructure vulnerabilities, security protocols, and processes and recommended changes to improve security. The work of this committee has led to the establishment of several key intradepartmental groups to tackle very specific security issues.

In addition, DOT spearheaded the establishment of a Container Working Group, established through the NISC in December. The Container Working Group is co-chaired with the U.S. Customs Service and includes representatives from the Departments of Defense, Energy, Commerce, Justice, Agriculture, Health and Human Services (Food and Drug Administration), and others. The Office of Homeland Security provides coordination and oversight for this initiative.

Working Together with the Office of Homeland Security and Federal, State, and Local Agencies

The challenge to improve our homeland security requires a coordinated effort among state, and local government agencies, as well as the private sector. Communication among these entities is key to assisting our officials at all levels to protect and defend against future terrorist attacks, and to effectively manage incidents should they occur.

To help meet these needs, the administration has implemented a uniform national threat advisory system to inform federal agencies, state and local officials, as well as the private sector, of terrorist threats and appropriate protective actions. The president's budget for fiscal year (FY) 2003 supports this effort by funding the development and implementation of secure information systems to streamline the dissemination of critical homeland security information. The department is requesting funding to upgrade its current Crisis Management Center into a new Transportation Information Operations Center (TIOC). The proposed TIOC will be the centralized information center for the Department of Transportation and will serve as the secretary's information center. The proposed TIOC will be a "24 hours per day, 7 days per week" center that will collect, analyze, and distribute information pertaining to the impacts of natural or human-made disasters, national security

---

The department must consider the law's tight deadlines as promises made to the American people.

---

related events, and special events and incidents as they affect transportation infrastructure and systems.

We are working with the states, airport authorities, and local governments as TSA transitions to a federal workforce of screeners and law enforcement personnel. In addition, we will be working with states, localities, and airports through the newly appointed federal security directors. The federal security directors are the frontline managers who will bring a standardized airport security system across America and will work with the public to ensure that airline passengers know in advance of new security procedures.

TSA will also rely on assistance from the states, airport authorities, and local law-enforcement agencies as it rolls out pilot programs to test security procedures. For instance, the State of Maryland is helping the TSA by supporting the use of the Baltimore-Washington International Airport as a laboratory site to study airport security operations, test TSA deployment techniques and technology, and pilot the deployment of the new screener workforce. This type of real-life coordinated support is key to our continued success.

Resource Requirements

As we continue to move forward in addressing the requirements established in the Aviation and Transportation Security Act, I have focused my efforts intensively on complying with or exceeding the deadlines established in the new law. In my view, the department must consider the law's tight deadlines as promises made to the American people, and we will do everything possible to keep these promises.

Thanks to the support of the president and the Congress, the department received nearly $2 billion in supplemental appropriations in the aftermath of the September 11th events. As a result, we have been able to press forward on many fronts and have been able to make great strides in establishing TSA, making airports and aircraft more secure, and enhancing the Coast Guard's presence on our waterways. Also because of this support, I was able to announce the implementation of the Port Security Grants Program, from which TSA will distribute $93.3 million in grant money to seaports to finance port security assessments and the costs related to enhancing facility and operational security. These important achievements would not have been possible without the additional financial support you provided that has gotten us through the past seven months.

Now I must ask for your continued support in providing the resources we need to meet the continuing challenges before us during the remaining months of FY 2002 and in FY 2003. In March, the president requested $4.4 billion in FY 2002 supplemental funds to support the continuing operation of the Transportation Security Administration through FY 2002. Absent these additional resources, we will have to look further within the administration to develop options to ensure the availability of funds within existing authorities to maintain operations beyond the end of the month. The passage of the president's supplemental request is necessary for TSA to meet the remainder of its statutory obligations.

In addition, the same supplemental request includes $255 million for homeland and port security activities to be carried out by the U.S. Coast Guard, $19.3 million for the Federal Motor Carrier Safety Administration to strengthen motor carrier oversight at the U.S. land borders with Mexico and Canada, and $3.5 million to upgrade DOT's current Crisis Management Center into a new Transportation Information Operations Center. This center will serve as a point of contact for other federal, state, local, and industry groups and will ensure an efficient and coordinated response from the department in the event of future crises. These FY 2002 financial resources requests will be critical to achieving our goals and the deadlines Congress set for us for the remainder of the fiscal year.

Your support is also critical to our planning for FY 2003. Added emphasis on homeland security is reflected throughout the president's FY 2003 request for resources for personnel, technology, and equipment to meet transportation security challenges. In total, the FY 2003 president's request for DOT includes $8.6 billion in homeland security–related needs. This includes $4.8 billion for the first full year of operation for the Transportation Security Administration. In addition, funding is requested for the Coast Guard at a level that will enable this critical service to continue to provide its expanded operations required to meet our homeland security needs while maintaining its traditional safety and law enforcement missions. I look forward to working with this committee on the specific requirements as you consider our FY 2003 appropriations request.

I believe we are on the right path to success in strengthening our homeland security at this critical time in our nation's history. I am confident that with your continued support we will be able to provide all Americans with a safe, reliable, efficient, and secure transportation system. We owe this to the American people, and they will expect nothing less. I want to again thank you for your continued support of our department, and I would be happy to answer any questions.

Homeland Security: Tracking International Students in Higher Education—Progress and Issues Since 9/11[2]

Janis Sposato

Assistant deputy executive associate commissioner, Immigration Services Division, U.S. Immigration and Naturalization Service, 2002– ; B.A. in psychology, Mount Holyoke College; law degree, Columbia Law School; trial attorney, Criminal Division, Department of Justice; special assistant to assistant attorney general, Civil Division; attorney adviser, Office of Legal Counsel; general counsel for the Justice Management Division; deputy assistant attorney general for law and policy, Justice Management Division; acting assistant attorney general for administration, 2001–2002.

Editors' introduction: After the terrorist attacks on the United States on September 11, 2001, the U.S. Immigration and Naturalization Service (INS) began developing a new system for tracking and monitoring some 550,000 foreign students and 275,000 exchange program visitors issued visas to the United States. The deadline for implementing that system was January 2003. Members of Congress and academic researchers, however, questioned the readiness of the new initiative and whether it would be installed on schedule. Ms. Sposato assured the Subcommittees on Select Education and 21st-Century Competitiveness of the House of Representatives that they would meet that date and claimed the new procedures would enable "us to keep our eyes open for and track those who may come to America for the wrong reason, while extending a hand in friendship to those seeking the knowledge that this great country has to offer."

Janis Sposato's testimony: Mr. Chairman and members of the committee, I am Janis Sposato, assistant deputy executive associate commissioner for Immigration Services Division (ISD).

Thank you for the opportunity to update the committee on the considerable progress the Immigration and Naturalization Service (INS) has made in implementing a new system that will greatly enhance our ability to track and monitor foreign students and

---

2. Delivered on September 24, 2002, 2:00 P.M., 2175 Rayburn House Office Building, at Washington, D.C.

exchange program visitors, progress that leaves us confident that we will meet the congressionally mandated deadline for full implementation.

This Internet-based system, known as the Student and Exchange Visitor Information System (SEVIS), will maintain critical, up-to-date information about foreign students and exchange visitors, and their dependents, and will allow for electronic access to this information. As such, it will enable the INS to track students in the United States more accurately and more expeditiously.

Introduction and Background

The INS is exerting greater control over the institutions authorized to admit foreign students in F and M visa status. The INS believes that for this brand new SEVIS system, review of all schools is the best method to ensure integrity. To facilitate the review of all INS-approved schools and to ensure the enrollment of all eligible schools in SEVIS in a timely manner, the INS has implemented a two-phased process for school review and SEVIS enrollment. Phase 1 was a preliminary enrollment period in which schools that have been INS-approved for at least the last three years to admit foreign students and are recognized as accredited or Title IV by the Department of Education were reviewed and granted access to SEVIS. Phase 2 will involve the certification of a school after a full review, including an on-site visit in many cases. For some schools, the on-site visit will verify their bona fides, but more importantly, the on-site visit will help ensure record-keeping and reporting compliance, as well as confirm that the schools are aware of their responsibilities. An interim rule that will explain the school certification process will be published in the near future.

> *The INS is exerting greater control over the institutions authorized to admit foreign students.*

The INS began accepting and reviewing school petitions for eligibility (Form I-17) in SEVIS as of July 1. As of September 11, 2002, there were 1,921 schools currently in various stages in the system. On July 15, 2002, the INS began enrolling and granting full SEVIS access to schools that submitted an electronic petition and that meet the preliminary enrollment criteria. That means that as of September 11, 736 schools were issuing and updating student records electronically in SEVIS. Also since that date, 595 schools had completed and submitted an electronic petition and were awaiting approval to use SEVIS. Another 590 schools created and saved drafts of such petitions but had not yet submitted a completed petition for adjudication. Upon approval, these schools will be able to access SEVIS to create and update student records.

SEVIS is part of an overall tightening of foreign student procedures and rules that INS is undertaking. Back in April, the INS published an interim rule that prohibits B nonimmigrant visitor visa holders from attending school prior to obtaining approval of a change to student status. Another proposed rule published in the *Federal Register* would, for example, prohibit aliens from changing from visitor status to student status unless they declared that intention at the time of visa issuance or admission to the United States. We are currently in the process of drafting that final rule.

Although the INS has improved many aspects of the overall foreign student program in the last months, the major focus of our efforts has been towards implementation of SEVIS. SEVIS enables schools and exchange visitor program sponsors to transmit electronic information and event notifications, via the Internet, to the INS and the Department of State (DOS) throughout a student's or exchange visitor's stay in the United States. Schools and exchange programs will update certain new information in SEVIS including, but not limited to, changes of address, program extensions, employment notifications, and changes in program of study. SEVIS will also provide system alerts and reports to the schools and exchange visitor program sponsors, as well as to INS and DOS offices.

How SEVIS Works

SEVIS, as a fully implemented system, will be an integrated system that incorporates information directly from schools, exchange programs, several INS systems, and the DOS. Before moving onto specifics about the progress made thus far, and the further development efforts already under way, I would like to give you an overview of the student process as it will work once SEVIS implementation is complete on January 1, 2003.

A prospective foreign student or exchange visitor first applies for admission to a school or acceptance by an exchange program sponsor. If accepted, the school or exchange program sponsor accesses SEVIS to input the data and to issue a Form I-20 or Form DS-2019. Therefore, at the time any Form I-20 or DS-2019 is printed, the information is entered into the SEVIS database. It is important to point out that prospective student in M, F, or J status may have applied to and been accepted by more than one U.S. institution and therefore may have more than one Form I-20 or DS-2019. After the foreign student or exchange visitor decides which school to attend, he or she will apply to a United States consulate or embassy to submit an application for a student or exchange visitor visa. During the visa screening process, the DOS officer will have access to SEVIS data to help verify the information and validate the Form I-20 or DS-2019. If the visa is approved, visa data is sent by the DOS to INS and Customs systems, and is updated in SEVIS. At the point of visa issuance, any Forms I-20 or DS-2019 that may have been issued to the foreign student by other schools become invalid and will be deactivated in SEVIS.

The foreign student or exchange visitor arrives at a U.S. port-of-entry. As the student or exchange visitor is inspected and admitted, the INS port-of-entry system will provide entry data to SEVIS, which will then be available to the school to notify them that a foreign student intending to attend their school is in the country and should be reporting for class. The student will then arrive at the school and register for class. Once the student has physically reported and enrolled, the school will report and update SEVIS, confirming arrival. If a foreign student fails to enroll, the student's SEVIS record will be terminated as out of status and notice will be provided to INS investigative and enforcement offices. If the student has properly enrolled, any changes in address, name, course of study, employment, transfers, and other monitored events should be reported by the student to the school's responsible officer, who will update SEVIS. If the student decides to continue studies at a higher academic level, for instance, a progression from undergraduate to a master's program, tracking will continue in SEVIS. Once the foreign student graduates, completes his or her current program or any practical training, the foreign student should depart the United States and return to his or her home country or, in accordance with U.S. law, change to another immigration status. As you can see, we are moving with SEVIS toward a

---

We are moving . . . toward a system that provides a more accurate and up-to-date picture of a foreign student's stay in the United States.

---

system that provides a more accurate and up-to-date picture of a foreign student's stay in the United States.

SEVIS Current Status

The INS issued a proposed rule on May 16, 2002, to implement SEVIS and to address foreign student processes and procedures. This rule was open for a thirty-day comment period, which closed on June 17, 2002. Under the proposed rule, SEVIS participation by all schools enrolling foreign students will become mandatory by January 30, 2003. The INS completed its review and analysis of the 152 comments, and a final rule has been drafted and is in the clearance process.

We have finalized what is generally referred to as "batch" technical specifications, which provides an optional method for the schools to report large volumes of data, system-to-system. In 2001 and 2002, INS sponsored SEVIS technical conferences for vendors, designated school officials, school representatives, and the public. These conferences were supplemented by another public technical conference on June 13, 2002, in Washington, D.C. Since that conference, upon the request of the American Council on Education (ACE), the INS delayed final posting of the batch technical details in order to meet with ACE and the Postsecondary Education Standards Council (PESC) for one last comment and review opportunity. In fact, we were able to incorporate some of their recommendations into the final version of the batch SEVIS Interface Control Document, which was posted for public availability on August 15, 2002. Batch functionality will be available for SEVIS schools to utilize this fall.

In addition to ACE, the INS interfaces regularly with NAFSA: Association of International Educators. In addition, the INS has met with other groups, including the American Association of Collegiate Registrars and Admissions Officers (AACRAO), the National Association of State Universities and Land-Grant Colleges (NASULGC), the National Association for Equal Opportunity in Higher Education (NAFEO), and the National Association of College and University Business Officers (NACUBO). For the last year INS had regularly scheduled SEVIS seminars across the country to provide the information necessary to schools and programs to begin implementation of SEVIS. With the publication of the proposed rule and the deployment of the system in July, INS transitioned from providing informational seminars to providing a SEVIS-dedicated national call center with multiple tiers to answer technical and policy-related questions. Furthermore, SEVIS staff still frequently participate in conferences at national and regional level educational conferences. INS is also publishing its third issue of *SEVIS—Smart*, a newsletter with updated information on the student and exchange visitor program. The newsletter, along with current policy memos, proposed regulations, frequently-asked-questions, and technical specifications are posted on the SEVIS public Web page (*www.ins.gov/graphics/services/tempbenefits/sevp.htm*), all in an effort to provide the community with the most up-to-date and accurate information. The most recent effort toward outreach involves the production of a SEVIS training video that was taped during a live broadcast involving 108 community colleges in the California educational system. The tape will be transferred to DVD and will be available to educational organizations to be used for their own training needs.

We are confident that we will meet the January 1, 2003, date established by the U.S.A. PATRIOT Act for making SEVIS available. Our proposed rule, and our present plan, is to require schools to begin using SEVIS for all new I-20s issued after January 30, 2003. In fact, we have deployed the initial operational version of SEVIS six months prior to the U.S.A. PATRIOT Act deadline. The INS will continue to enroll schools and is working aggressively to enhance SEVIS toward full implementation. The $36.8 million appropriation provided by the Congress in the Counter-Terrorism Supplemental has facilitated the development and implementation of the system.

Continuing Efforts Towards Full Implementation of SEVIS

The INS is working toward enhancing our data share arrangement with the DOS Office of Consular Affairs in order to electronically provide SEVIS data for verification during the visa issuance process. INS and DOS currently have a Nonimmigrant Visa (NIV) Datashare arrangement, whereby DOS is sending all nonimmigrant visa issuance data to INS and Customs systems. SEVIS plans to extract data of all the F (academic), M (vocational), and J (exchange visitor) records from that existing arrangement.

The SEVIS program staff have been working closely with the INS Entry/Exit program staff in order to collect data, such as date and port of entry as mandated by the U.S.A. PATRIOT Act. SEVIS has been included in the functional requirements for phase 1 of a comprehensive entry/exit system. Phase 1 consists of the Visa Waiver Permanent Program Act (VWPPA) Support System, which leverages existing information technology systems, specifically the Advance Passenger Information System (APIS) and the Arrival Departure Information System (ADIS) to capture data electronically. This first phase of the entry/exit system will provide entry data on all F, M, and J aliens to SEVIS at all air and sea ports-of-entry. For those ports-of-entry not yet included in the entry/exit system, we will have alternative processes to provide data to SEVIS and notice to the schools.

Significant Events Affecting SEVIS

The strides that we have made and the plans for further development of SEVIS have been, in part, shaped by a number of recent events. I would like to note some of these events, to provide greater context for our achievements.

On October 29, 2001, the president directed the secretary of state and the attorney general, in conjunction with other relevant departments and agencies, to develop a program to strengthen international student processes. The president reaffirmed the importance of tracking international students and exchange visitors and called for the INS to conduct periodic reviews of institutions certified to enroll foreign students and exchange visitors to ensure school compliance with record-keeping and reporting requirements. The INS is implementing the president's guidance through the implementation of SEVIS, and the review and certification of schools during the SEVIS enrollment process.

On May 14, 2002, the Enhanced Border Security and Visa Entry Reform Act (Border Security Act) of 2002 was signed into law. In addition to addressing information collection, updates, and reporting elements, the Border Security Act requires schools to report the failure of a foreign student to enroll within 30 days after their registration deadline. The INS has established a toll-free, 1-800 number for schools to report a foreign student's failure to enroll, and once all schools are enrolled they will be able to report directly in SEVIS. The INS is also required by this legislation to review all schools every two years to ensure compliance with record-keeping and reporting requirements.

On May 20, 2002, the Department of Justice's Office of the Inspector General (IG) issued a report entitled *The Immigration and Naturalization Service's Contacts with Two September 11 Terrorists: A Review of the INS's Admissions of Mohammed Atta and Marwan Alshehhi, Its Processing of Their Change of Status Applications, and Its Efforts to Track Foreign Students in the United States*. Sections of this report identified deficiencies in the foreign student process and made recommendations, many of which were already being planned or implemented by the INS. The report also questioned INS's ability to meet the SEVIS implementation deadlines. As I testify today, we believe we are on track to disprove the IG's finding. Further, through our timely implementation of SEVIS, the INS will have addressed many, if not all, of the concerns raised by the IG regarding student tracking.

Conclusion

Mr. Chairman, full implementation of SEVIS will revise and enhance the process by which foreign students and exchange visitors gain admission to the United States. The INS, through SEVIS, will increase its ability to track and monitor foreign students and exchange visitors in order to ensure that they arrive in the United States, show up and register at the school or exchange visitor program, and properly maintain their status during their stay as valued guests in this country. SEVIS better enables us to keep our eyes open for and track those who may come to America for the wrong reason, while extending a hand in friendship to those seeking the knowledge that this great country has to offer. Implementing SEVIS will allow our nation to strike the proper balance between openness to international students and exchange visitors and the security obtained by enforcing our nation's laws.

"To Provide for the Common Defense"[3]

Hillary Rodham Clinton

U.S. senator from New York, 2001– ; born Chicago, IL, October 26, 1947, and raised in Park Ridge, IL, attending public schools there; B.A.,Wellesley College, 1969; J.D., Yale Law School, 1973; attorney, Children's Defense Fund, 1973–74; assistant professor of law, University of Arkansas, 1974–77; partner, Rose Law Firm, 1977–92; lecturer, University of Arkansas Law School, 1979–80; in Senate, member of committees on Budget, Environment and Public Works, Health, Education, Labor, and Pension, and Armed Services; author, It Takes a Village and Other Lessons Children Teach Us (1996); Claude Pepper Award of the National Association for Home Care, Martin Luther King, Jr., Award of the Progressive National Baptist Convention, and Public Spirit Award of the American Legion Auxiliary.

Editors' introduction: After terrorists killed thousands of Americans and others from some 80 countries on September 11, 2001, President Bush created a new cabinet-level Department of Homeland Security on January 24, 2003, that drew criticism from many corners. One of those critics was Senator Clinton, who, in a speech at John Jay College of Criminal Justice, expressed her concern that "our approach to securing our nation is haphazard at best" and urged the Bush administration to pass the Provide for the Common Defense Act which she believed would help to improve security within the U.S.

Hillary Rodham Clinton's speech: In the months following September 11th, a new reality took hold in every corner of our country. We saw the National Guard in our airports and in front of government buildings. Bioterrorism and weapons of mass destruction were talked about at kitchen tables and in classrooms all across America. The skies over New York and Washington, D.C., were patrolled by our military.

   And nearly every American came to believe that we were taking bold steps to guard against terrorist attacks and make our nation safe.

---

3. Delivered on January 24, 2003, at New York City.

But time has passed and our vigilance has faded. Not at the front lines here at home, where our police, firefighters, and emergency response personnel remain alert. Not at the front lines overseas, where our men and women in uniform are serving to defend us every day.

Our vigilance has faded at the top, in the corridors of power in Washington, D.C., where the strategy and resources to protect our nation are supposed to originate. Where leaders are supposed to lead.

Our constitutional imperative, to "provide for the common defense," has not been fully realized. As a result, our people remain vulnerable, nearly as vulnerable as they were before 8:46 A.M. on September 11. And here in New York, that complacency doesn't just threaten our security, it tears at our hearts.

Here we are, gathered in the city that lost nearly 3,000 lives—343 were firefighters and EMTs, and 60 were police officers. We can never forget what the first responders did. With no thought about their own safety, they rescued tens of thousands of lives. And in the aftermath, they stayed, searching until every square inch of Ground Zero was covered.

> *Our consti-*
> *tutional*
> *imperative,*
> *to "provide*
> *for the*
> *common*
> *defense," has*
> *not been*
> *fully*
> *realized.*

Some of the same men and women who symbolized America's resolve on its darkest day are in this room. We're glad you are here, thankful for your service.

Yet, some of you face the unbelievable threat of losing your jobs. Would we dare do this to our military forces overseas? Would we dare pull army and navy officers out of duty in the Persian Gulf and force them into retirement? Would we strip the marines or the air force of planes or equipment that they need to confront Al Qaeda or Iraq? Of course not; and yet, that is precisely what will be happening to the men and women and resources we need here at the front lines of our homeland defense.

While today, the new Department of Homeland Security opens its doors in Washington, D.C., here at this conference, we are examining the question of how far has our nation come since September 11th when it comes to homeland security. What has been done, and what is left to be done? Where are we now, and where do we go from here?

The truth is we are not prepared, we are not supporting our first responders, and our approach to securing our nation is haphazard at best. We have relied on a myth of homeland security—a myth written in rhetoric, inadequate resources, and a new bureaucracy, instead of relying on good old fashion American ingenuity, might, and muscle.

I believe we need to get this nation back on the right track when it comes to domestic preparedness. We need a similar kind of mobilization that happened after Pearl Harbor to strengthen our domestic defense. We need new, comprehensive, and focused policy initiatives, like the legislation I will propose today. And we need to find out where our homeland security money is going because, as the survey I will release today will show, it is not getting to most of our cities and towns.

Homeland security is not simply about reorganizing existing bureaucracies. It is about having the right attitude, focus, policy, and resources, and right now we are lacking in all four.

Soon after the planes hit the towers, the Pentagon, and crashed in the field in Pennsylvania, commentators and citizens described these tragic attacks as our generation's Pearl Harbor. And despite the differences, there is something to that comparison, especially in the way the date stands out so starkly in our minds, and always will. And especially in the way people felt in the aftermath of these surprise attacks; we felt like W. H. Auden wrote, "For nothing now can ever come to any good."

And yet, because we are Americans, some good did come when we rose up and conquered fascism. And in our time, we have defeated the Taliban and put Al Qaeda on the defensive.

But the comparison stops just when it should continue. Within weeks of the attack on Pearl Harbor, blackout shades were in every window along the East Coast. Yellow sirens lined the West Coast to warn of a possible Japanese attack. Searchlights shot to the sky from Bryant Park, and Times Square dimmed its great white way. People signed up for military service in droves. A sleeping giant awoke, and marched to victory in 1945.

President Franklin D. Roosevelt was clear about what America needed to accomplish in order to fight the war. He called for factories and workers to double their production of guns, tanks, and munitions, and he drafted all able men. In fireside chats, he prepared the country for the long road to victory. And the American people responded to FDR's forthright call for sacrifice.

Soon the effort on the home front was just as great as the effort on the western front. Americans rationed gasoline, meat, and butter. They recycled rubber and metal. Victory gardens produced 40 percent of the vegetables consumed at home. Six million women went to work in our factories. The American worker accepted lower wages to keep inflation down. And civil defense was in every village, town, and city. This focused effort prepared our nation and produced our victory against the original Axis.

New York's Mayor La Guardia was appointed the head of the Office of Civil Defense. Out of concern that the draft was taking so many police and firefighters, he called for volunteers to keep the city safe. He said, "The war will come right to our streets and residential districts." He was right; it just didn't happen for another 60 years. And "over there" has finally come over here.

After September 11th, the concept of war was forever changed. The battlefield is now anywhere at anytime, the front lines are at our front doors, and we now have veterans and casualties of the war on terrorism.

Do we need to ration? Of course not. Do we need victory gardens? No. And no one has to accept a lower wage to fend off inflation. Times have changed and because of our new technologies and advancements, we do not need to imitate exactly what the Greatest Generation did. But we do need to imitate how they felt and how quickly and forcefully they responded to the new threat our nation faced. We do need more of that same attitude. We need to meet the challenges to our freedom with resources, attitude, ideas, and focus.

We have of course made some progress. Our military forces have fought bravely and successfully overseas. Airports are more secure. The improved information sharing between the FBI and local law enforcement helped capture the terrorist cell outside Buffalo. We hired 750 more food inspectors as part of a $3.2 billion effort to combat bioterrorism. My hardworking colleague Senator Schumer secured $150 million for port security and to improve technologies that could detect nuclear bombs in cargo containers on ships and trucks headed for American ports and border crossings. And we all know that New York City is on the road to recovery.

We need to meet the challenges to our freedom with resources, attitude, ideas, and focus.

While these accomplishments matter, they are nowhere near enough. And today when people ask "Are we safer today than we were on the morning of September 11, 2001?" The answer is only marginally, because somewhere along the line, we lost our edge. We let our guard down.

Now is the time to renew our sense of purpose in a way that mirrors what happened after Pearl Harbor.

The very first thing I did when this new session of Congress began was to reintroduce the Homeland Security Block Grant Act, which will provide more than $3 billion in direct funding to our communities and local police, fire, and emergency responders. It was my first order of business in this new Congress because America's first responders should be first on our domestic security agenda.

But in working with mayors, fire commissioners, police chiefs, and other emergency workers on this legislation, I heard over and over again that they do not have the resources they need to protect America.

So I conducted a survey to get at the question: Just how much federal funding for homeland security is really getting to our communities? We reached out to every town, village, city, and county in New York State—from Westchester to Rochester—that would be eligible to receive funding under my Block Grant bill and do you know what we found? Of the forty counties and municipalities that responded, a full 70 percent have said that they have not received any homeland security funding. Not one single penny.

One of the most striking findings is the extent to which communities tried to improve their preparedness levels without sufficient resources, though many respondents conveyed that this could not continue without significant federal assistance. Since September 11th, cities and towns have answered the call to increase our defenses at home, investing more than $2.6 billion from their own budgets in the name of homeland security.

In Buffalo, they spent $465,000 responding to every possible anthrax scare. Extra security personnel were hired to protect Buffalo Niagara International Airport for $843,000. There are new costs to protect the city's water system—$366,000. And because of the lack of funding, 97 police positions were lost and two fire companies were closed.

In Yonkers, they have incurred more than $109,000 in building security costs, $57,000 to purchase new protective suits, storage

---

We expect people and cities and towns to react to oranges, reds, and yellows, but we do not give them the green light they need to do their jobs.

---

units for anthrax evidence, and $61,000 for additional police officers assigned to City Hall. And in 2003, they need more than $250,000 to cover additional security measures.

The City of Albany spent $368,000 on first responder overtime costs, $40,000 on gas masks for the police department, $1.5 million to protect three reservoirs that provide water to the capital region, and $3.7 million to purchase equipment that would help it better detect biological and chemical agents in the Loudenville reservoir.

Every day our public servants from Binghamton to Buffalo to Brooklyn are sacrificing to secure every corner of this country. But every day, despite some of our efforts, we do less and less for them. We expect people and cities and towns to react to oranges, reds, and yellows, but we do not give them the green light they need to do their jobs. It is too bad that the people who issue the warnings to our cities aren't the same people who write the checks to cover their costs.

Even New York City, which was the most prepared city in America on September 11th, still has a lot to do. Since September 11th, NYC has dedicated 1,000 police officers to counterterrorism and intelligence. In order to purchase better emergency equipment for police officers, firefighters, and public hospitals, they need more than $189 million; $99 million is needed for first responder training. It will take more than $223 million to improve communications equipment. The bottom line: According to the city's own estimates, New York City needs more than $900 million in order protect this city and respond to a future attack.

But sadly, the administration is holding up valuable resources that New York City and so many other cities and towns across America need. They have delayed $1.5 billion that was supposed to go immediately to first responders. And back in August, the president refused to designate as an emergency $2.5 billion for homeland security costs.

Adding insult to injury, last week Congress had a choice. As many of you know, Senator Byrd, both last year and this year, has been a stalwart fighter for homeland security funds, holding hearings to find out what America needs and imploring our colleagues to meet those needs. Last week, we could have passed the Byrd amendment that had $585 million for port security, $150 million to purchase interoperable radios so our police, firefighters, and emergency service workers can communicate effectively, and another $83 million to protect our borders, but in each case Congress settled for less.

Yes, you heard correctly—Congress settled for less. Can you imagine our predecessors in the Congress in 1942 or 1943 doing such a thing?

As I said earlier, homeland security is about attitude, focus, policy, and resources. We need a new attitude, a more intense focus, serious comprehensive policy, and adequate resources to do the job right. We need to move beyond the piecemeal approach, and we cannot continue to operate under the illusion that simply putting a new name on an old building fixes the problem. That is why today I am announcing the Provide for the Common Defense Act.

The Provide for the Common Defense Act does four main things:

- First, it establishes a Public-Private Security Task Force, within the Department of Homeland Security, that would work with industry leaders and security experts to help develop minimum security standards for certain industry sectors to follow. I know that many industries have already voluntarily taken on this task, and we need to learn from them. Those that make up our nation's critical infrastructure, including telecommunications, energy, banking, finance, and transportation, would have one year to develop adequate standards on a voluntary basis. If they do not, the federal government would assume that responsibility.

  For example, I have already introduced legislation to strengthen security at our nation's nuclear power plants and chemical plants. Because when it comes to security, it is in everyone's interest, owners and operators included, to secure our nation's critical infrastructure. But while it is in everyone's interest, at the end of the day, it is the federal government's responsibility, to make sure standards are set and maintained.

- Second, the Provide for the Common Defense Act moves America beyond the Cold War era when it comes to research and development. Of the federal government's investment in combating terrorism, only 5 percent of those resources have been dedicated to research and development. And we know that our investment in nonmilitary, nonhealth-related R and D has decreased by 0.02 percent since September 11. This bill ensures that there is a "Counterterror Technology Fund," a central dedicated funding source for major new investments in promising technology.

- Third, this bill provides extra attention to our most vulnerable regions. As we in New York know all too well, certain places are more appealing targets because of the American values they represent or because they are densely populated. The Homeland Security Act provided a coordinator for the Washington, D.C., metropolitan region but not for the New York metropolitan region. Senator Schumer and I believe that we need this office and that we can correct this inconsistency by providing a coordinator for the tri-state area and requiring vulnerability assessments of our nation's ten most populated metropolitan regions.

  Similarly, this legislation aims to correct the disparity in attention paid to our northern and southern borders. According to a July 2001 report from the Justice Department, only 4 percent of border patrol agents work along the U.S.–Canadian border—that means 96 percent of the agents patrol the southern border. While there have been some improvements, they are not enough, so I believe we need to designate a northern border coordinator within the Homeland Security Department.

- Fourth and finally, we need to create more than a department, we need to create a deterrent. We want to show the terrorists that if they attack, we're prepared. We will not be caught off guard. We want to send a message that while they might break our hearts by taking away our loved ones, they will not break our spirit and take away the lives we lead as Americans. We can do this by filling some of the major gaps left by September 11th, like tracking the health of the first soldiers in this new war who lived and worked and volunteered at Ground Zero and coordinating our relief services in a national 2-1-1 line.

So, in taking the broad and long view of homeland security, the Provide for the Common Defense Act establishes a Public-Private Task Force to develop minimum security standards, sets the stage for progress and investment with a Counterterror Technology Fund, pays special attention to our most vulnerable regions, and aims to deter future attacks.

By providing for our common defense, we make a common commitment as a nation, as leaders, and as private citizens to do all that we can to make September 11th the only day of infamy for this generation.

The good news is there is no shortage of ideas to improve our domestic defense. The bad news is that few of these ideas have become the law of the land. And that's a dangerous thing. Because rhetoric won't stop the spread of anthrax or smallpox. Rhetoric won't help the Coast Guard track ships that are carrying dangerous cargo. Rhetoric won't secure our chemical and nuclear power plants. We need to put our best ideas into practice and back them with resources.

Unfortunately, the main idea to come out of the administration in recent weeks is to eliminate the tax on dividends—at a cost of $364 billion. Will ending the dividend tax make air travel safer? Will it secure our nuclear power plants? Will it keep a dirty bomb out of New York harbor?

Will ending the tax on dividends save one police officer or firefighter his or her job?

In short, will it make America safer, more secure?

Of course, the answer is no.

Around the world, terrorist attacks continue. More than 200 people died in the Bali bombings. American servicemen were killed in Kuwait. Al Qaeda blew up a French destroyer in Yemen. A car bomb in Kenya killed 14 tourists, and a shoulder-launched missile by the grace of God missed a plane carrying more than 200 people to Israel. It is very possible that Osama bin Laden is alive, and that Al Qaeda and even other organizations are plotting all the while.

We cannot secure our nation without a renewed focus and vigilance like we had in those weeks and months after that tragic day in September. Even though some of the flags have come down from windows and no longer wave on front lawns, I still believe that the American people are prepared to make sacrifices, if need be, to secure our nation. They are patriots, and I believe that if they are asked, they too will answer the call.

Now is the time to adjust our attitude, our focus, our policies, and our resources to fit our new reality. Now is the time to Provide for our Common Defense. And we need only look to our nation's own history to see how this can be done.

Next week, Americans will gather around their televisions to listen to President Bush's State of the Union address. On February 23, 1942, Americans gathered around their radios to listen to President Roosevelt's call to arms and for the nation to sacrifice for the greater good. He said, "Never before have we been called upon for such a prodigious effort. Never before have we had so little time in which to do so much." Those words are as true today as they were then, and we ignore their wisdom at our own peril.

Safe and Sound: Strengthening American Security Today[4]

Joseph Lieberman

U.S. senator from Connecticut, 1988– ; born and raised Stamford, CT, February 24, 1942; bachelor's degree, Yale College, 1964; law degree, Yale Law School, 1967; Connecticut State Senate, 1970–80; private legal practice, 1981–82; attorney general, Connecticut, 1982–88; Democratic candidate for vice president, 2000; candidate for nomination by Democratic Party for president of the U.S., 2003– ; ranking member and former chairman, Senate Governmental Affairs Committee; member, Environment and Public Works, Armed Services, and Small Business Committees; former chairman, Democratic Leadership Committee (DLC); author The Power Broker *(1966),* Scorpion and the Tarantula *(1970), and* Child Support in America *(1986).*

Editors' introduction: After September 11, 2001, when terrorists killed thousands of Americans and citizens from some 80 other countries in New York, Washington, D.C., and Pennsylvania, politicians, members of think tanks, and others speculated as to how best to protect the United States from future attacks. Addressing a forum sponsored by the ANSER Institute for Homeland Security and the Elliott School for International Affairs at George Washington University, Senator Lieberman, candidate for nomination by the Democratic Party for president, questioned the Bush administration's "national resolve" when funding programs needed to provide for the nation's safety. Insisting that "we remain in too much danger today," the senator recommended attending to "three homeland security needs that have not yet been adequately addressed." Begun in California in 1958, the ANSER Institute, whose home office is in Arlington, Virginia, strives to lead the debate for national security through executive-level education, public awareness programs, workshops for policy makers, and online publications. Senator Lieberman was introduced by the president of George Washington University, Stephen Joel Trachtenberg.

Joseph Lieberman's speech: Thank you, President Trachtenberg.

---

4. Delivered on February 14, 2003, at Washington, D.C.

Ever since 1958—when our country was in the midst of a very different kind of conflict against a very different kind of foe—ANSER has informed and improved the common defense. You've seen around corners as the road we're traveling has taken unexpected turns—and helped America remain secure. And the Elliott School, in just fourteen years, has built on GW's long history of leadership in international affairs—with a strong sense of the current challenges we face and a clear vision for the future.

These have been difficult days for Americans' sense of security at home. Last week, the terror alert rose to code orange. This week we heard bin Laden's voice on the tape, calling again for his followers to kill. Combined with warnings from the directors of the FBI and CIA that another terrorist attack on America could occur as early as "this week"—and urgings from other officials for Americans to create safe rooms in their homes and buy three days' supply of food and water—that has understandably heightened the anxiety of millions of people.

And the fact is, this administration has not made homeland security the funding priority it must be.

David McIntyre, deputy director of the ANSER Institute for Homeland Security, perfectly framed the question this way: "Will orange become the color of confusion and fear, or the color of national resolve? We can decide."

Looking back at the Bush administration's record on homeland defense, over the 17 months that have passed since September 11th, 2001, I do not see "the color of national resolve." The administration has been too slow, too protective of the status quo, and too unwilling to back up tough talk with real resources when it comes to improving our homeland defenses. As a result, we remain in too much danger today. Our borders and ports are too porous, our first responders are under-supported, our infrastructure is under-protected, and our supply of vaccines and antidotes is far too limited. We can and must do better.

The best measure of the problem is the budget the administration just put forward. This is more than a statement of accounting. It's a statement of the nation's priorities, a statement of our values. And the fact is, this administration has not made homeland security the funding priority it must be.

In a time of war—facing a fierce and ruthless enemy that targets us here at home as well as overseas—this administration would spend far more of our national treasure on ineffective and unfair tax cuts than on homeland security. The proposed budget recommends total homeland security spending of $41.3 billion for the next fiscal year, an increase of only about $300 million—or less than 1 percent over what the administration approved for homeland security for this year. But at the same time the budget would have us spend $102 billion—more than 300 times that amount—to enact tax cuts next year, on the way to $695 billion in new tax cuts over the next 10 years.

Leadership is about choices as well as intentions. And this administration is not putting its leadership and our money where our needs are. Its choices favor the wallets of the few over the safety of us all. This is not a matter of opinion. It is a matter of fact, in the black and white of this budget.

America has the greatest military in the world because we pay for it. If we want the best domestic defenses, we'll have to pay for them, too. But consider this comparison. Between this year's and next year's budgets, the administration recommends increased defense spending of $19 billion. I will support that increase. But over the same period, the administration only thinks we need $300 million more to improve our homeland defenses, which are far less prepared to protect our people today than the Pentagon is.

Homeland security demands many times the $300 million increase this administration proposes. After extensive review and consultation with many independent experts, I have determined that at a minimum, to meet our urgent homeland security needs, we need to invest $16 billion more than the president proposes for our homeland security—including $7.5 billion more than the president wants for our local first responders. I ask the Congress and the president to work together to provide these additional resources.

We must rise above rote partisanship and rigid ideology and put America's homeland security first.

And next year's budget is only part of the problem. Before we start celebrating about the spending bill for this year that passed last night, let's make one thing clear. There is little new funding for local first responders in this year's budget. In this Code Orange status, our job now in Washington is to get the money that has been appropriated, which was tied up in the bureaucracy for far too long, out to local communities immediately—and at the same time, to turn our attention to securing desperately needed additional funds.

We are at war. Our local first responders are in need. We must act with urgency today.

These are not ordinary times, and they must not be met by ordinary politics. We have too many urgent priorities to meet. We must rise above rote partisanship and rigid ideology and put America's homeland security first.

That means investing more now—and deploying those resources swiftly and smartly. It is in that spirit today that I want to offer three proposals to meet three homeland security needs that have not yet been adequately addressed. I hope the White House and members of Congress will seriously consider these proposals and then join in supporting them.

1. A Frontline Initiative to Support First Responders

The single most glaring gap in federal leadership and support is for those who need it most. America's local firefighters, police officers, and emergency medical technicians are not getting the assistance they need to protect us in the war against terrorism.

That is shameful. Our 9 million first responders, who are on the front lines of our defense in the war on terrorism, need more than gratitude and moral support. They need real resources. But the administration is asking for the same $3.5 billion for first responders this year as it did last year. And even that is misleading—because the budget also proposes cutting funds for local law enforcement by 42 percent. The COPS program, which has hired more than 100,000 police officers, is being eviscerated by an 85 percent cut in support.

Today I am proposing an immediate Frontline Homeland Defense Initiative to get first responders the four things they most need now to stop terrorism: training, communications, information, and funding.

Funding. I've never believed that money alone solves a problem. But here we are trying to spearhead a vast new national effort to protect ourselves from an unprecedented new threat. That will take money. To buy new technology. To hire, support, and train professionals. To develop and deploy new vaccines and antidotes. To update computer networks and integrate communications systems.

In a recent U.S. Conference of Mayors study, three-quarters of mayors nationwide reported a funding shortfall for threat detection and emergency response equipment.

According to a top local official, Los Angeles needs more than $11 million this year alone to better prepare its first responders and $19 million for training to protect against weapons of mass destruction. Those are for immediate, stopgap measures—not long-term solutions.

To meet the urgent need for additional firefighters throughout America, we should pass the SAFER Act—which will provide $7 billion over six years to local communities to add thousands of additional firefighters who are needed in the war on terrorism. In some communities, the number of firefighters is actually being reduced because of the budget crises localities are facing. That couldn't come at a worse time.

State and local authorities desperately need better training. So today, I ask the Department of Homeland Security and Department of Defense to offer first responders throughout the country expanded access to special training by the U.S. military on chemical, biological, radiological, and nuclear weaponry, and expanded access to our military bases to receive that training. This hasn't happened—because, according to reports, the Defense Department is reluctant to foot the bill. It's time for the president to make it happen.

And to make sure that first responders and all counterterrorism professionals get the full range of skills they need for the future, I suggest the establishment of a National Homeland Security Academy under the new department—a kind of West Point for domestic defense to train the best and brightest future leaders.

First responders also need far more help communicating with one another. In New York on September 11th, we lost firefighters because their communications equipment wasn't compatible with what the police were using. A new federally financed study by the National Fire Protection Association shows the problem is widespread; only a quarter of our fire departments nationwide have equipment for easy communication with state and federal emergency response agencies.

The Public Safety Wireless Network, a joint Treasury and Justice Department policy group, has estimated the cost of replacing all state and local communications equipment nationwide to allow our first responders to talk to each other in a crisis to be $18 billion. That's a long-term figure, and not every single state, town, and city will necessarily need new equipment. But there's no question the

---

Local officials need to find out about threats rapidly and routinely from the feds—not from the headlines.

---

requirement is wide and serious. Communities around the country also need federal guidance, training, and standards to put their own communication plans in place and make their own investments. I would give them $4 billion in additional funds in next year's budget to help meet this communications challenge rapidly—as part of the $7.5 billion over the president's proposal that I recommend for first responders.

Our local law enforcement officers need swift and accurate information if they are to be effective first preventers as well as first responders. Now, they're at the short end of the sharing stick. Last October's Hart-Rudman report said that police officers on the beat are effectively operating "deaf, dumb, and blind."

Today I call on the administration to accelerate a Smart Intelligence Sharing Strategy to break through the antiquated barriers to information sharing between federal law enforcement and intelligence agencies and local first responders. Some of this is already in the Homeland Security Act signed by the president last December—but it just won't get done without clear direction from the White House.

Local officials need to find out about threats rapidly and routinely from the feds—not from the headlines. Today, they're being kept at arm's length. In October 2001, the federal government received a credible threat that a ten kiloton nuclear bomb was being smuggled into Manhattan and might be detonated—but not even Mayor Rudy Giuliani was told.

As we speak, local law enforcement officials are still not getting all the information they need about ongoing terrorism investigations in their jurisdictions, not to mention basic background information on terrorism. If we in Washington expect them to do their job effectively, we have to give them the tools and the information.

That means state and local police departments must get instant and integrated access to all 58 federal terrorist watch lists so that they can check those lists when making routine stops. And we should enact a recommendation of former senators Hart and Rudman and create a 24-hour operation center in each state to provide a real-time link between local and federal law enforcement.

The new information sharing strategy must also include an immediate overhaul of the security clearance process so that state and local officials have the status they need to do what their jobs—and our safety—demand. As of June 2002, secret clearance investigations took over 6 months to complete, and top-secret clearance investigations typically took between 12 and 18 months. There are some initial indications this has started to improve—but we need to drive hard for permanent progress. Bureaucratic barriers to local law enforcement and prevention breed danger for us all.

2. Shoring up Ports, Borders, and Transportation Systems

My second proposal is aimed at better protecting our ports, borders, and transportation networks.

As you probably know, less than 2 percent of all containers coming through our 361 ports are inspected. Far too much truck and rail traffic also comes into and across America without being scrutinized or scanned.

With the vast volume of merchandise passing through our ports and over our borders, we simply cannot inspect every container by hand. But we can use Customs officials and advanced technology to inspect containers before they might become a threat. The administration has started this work, but with inadequate funding, it's going too slowly.

We should work with the private sector to make sure that, beginning as close as possible to their point of origin, all containers have their contents verified and are securely sealed, and then are logged and tracked with a transponder.

And we must quickly shore up the physical security of our home ports. The Coast Guard has estimated that doing that—just adding guards, gates, and monitors—will cost about $4.4 billion, starting with a billion dollars this year. Industry will inevitably foot some of that bill. But so far the federal government has contributed a paltry $92 million—less than a tenth of this year's need and just 2 percent of the long-term cost. I will fight in Congress for $1.2 billion more for the physical security of our ports this year.

In the same way, at the same time, as the tide of danger rises, we can't maintain the pre–September 11th pace for modernizing our Coast Guard fleet. What was scheduled to take 20 years must now happen in 10 at most. To do that, we need to at least double the $500 million the president has requested for Coast Guard modernization next year.

So too, many now slip into America illegally with far too much ease. To plug the gaps, we need at least 2,000 to 3,000 additional border personnel, along with new technology to create smart borders. Together, these priorities will require at least $1 billion in additional funding in next year's budget.

What comes through our ports and over our borders gets right on our roads, rails, and other modes of transit. We've made progress since September 11th in safeguarding air travel. Luggage is being screened for explosives; air marshals are riding more flights; and armored cockpit doors are being installed—and will be on all domestic and U.S.–bound international planes by April.

But just as terrorists constantly change their means and mode of attack, the TSA must broaden its scope of defense—and rapidly. I challenge the administration to commit the real resources necessary to protect the roads, rails, bridges, tunnels, subways, and all other modes of transportation. TSA's appropriation is actually decreased in the president's budget for next year—which will make it difficult to keep pace with their current responsibilities, much less take on new ones. TSA needs an additional $1.7 billion in this budget to do the job we need it to do for our security.

3. Refocusing Our Armed Forces

Today around Washington, antiaircraft missiles have been deployed by the Pentagon. That will be a critical part of our homeland defense if our enemies use similar methods to the September 11th attack. This new terrorist age of danger demands a bold and comprehensive new strategy to systematically focus more of our mighty military's strength right here inside our borders.

We don't need to reinvent our military for this purpose, but we do need to do some redirecting and reengineering to meet the new homeland threats. Let me give you a few examples. Some capabilities—like medical units, detection and decontamination units, power generation and aviation units—may need to be increased. Others will need to be tailored. Antiaircraft missiles can guard more critical sites. Today, fewer combat aircraft patrol our skies than in the immediate aftermath of September 11th; perhaps more should now be dedicated to that task. And our military can help us develop better protocols for communication, medical response, and chemical, biological, and radiological decontamination of large areas and populations.

And as a part of this overall new effort, we should add domestic defense as one of the primary missions of our National Guard.

This should not overlap with the critical role of local police. The Guard and police have different strengths, expertise, and capabilities.

But in the immediate near-term, selected guard units can be dispatched to defend underdefended chemical plants, as well as biological and nuclear facilities. Their eyes, ears, minds, and muscle can protect those sites while we develop a longer term public-private security strategy.

In the months to come, careful planning can focus the Guard's strengths on addressing other major needs. For example, National Guard State Area Commands should help train local first responders in catastrophic response; and, in the event of another attack, Guard engineers must be ready to assist with rebuilding infrastructure, just as they currently do abroad.

Our government needs to provide clear and concrete guidance that ordinary Americans can act upon to help protect themselves.

To encourage young Americans to help us meet this challenge, I will introduce legislation to expand the ROTC and add domestic defense to its curriculum. Young Americans who enlist for service in one of the selected Guard units would get a special enlistment bonus, guaranteed homeland security training, and increased GI Bill entitlements to be used by themselves or any member of their immediate family.

Conclusion

Of course, strengthening our security in an age of terrorism is not government's job alone. We've been reminded in recent days that the warnings hit not just close to home—they literally go inside our homes. For most Americans, daily life has not changed much since September 11th. Now, duct tape and safe rooms tell us that we are a nation at war, and that, with inhumane enemies like Al Qaeda who want to harm us, we must change our lives if we are to stop them from changing our way of life.

Our government needs to provide clear and concrete guidance that ordinary Americans can act upon to help protect themselves. Checklists and videos, available for free in Post Offices and other public places, would prepare families, businesses, schools, congregations, and associations for every terror level and potential emergency. Secretary Ridge should go on network television one evening soon and talk us through the realities and possibilities of our current Code Orange threat. Professionals should advise parents what to tell their children. We shouldn't spread fear. We should clarify and educate.

This is a case where a little knowledge causes a lot of fear. A lot more knowledge might well reduce the fear and better prepare us all.

And we can and must go further to bring out the patriot in every American. Everywhere I go, I meet people hungry to help and to serve. In the months to come, I'll talk more about my vision of how we can better engage ordinary American citizens to protect ourselves and help us win this war.

But it all starts with leadership and resources from Washington. It all starts with the right priorities and the right choices from those of us privileged to lead. Lacking that, even the best intentions of millions of Americans cannot produce a safer nation or a more secure people.

Halfway around the world today, the American military is preparing to join with allies to disarm a dictator who has failed to comply with the will of the world. If we must fight, our victory will be decisive—and I know that when it is, the world will be a safer place. Here at home, to guard the land beneath our feet, the freedom that has defined America since the beginning, we are engaged in a different kind of war. One that we have been too slow and too miserly in organizing to fight.

We owe it to our nation and ourselves to do better. On September 3, 1939, shortly after Britain declared war on Germany, Winston Churchill said, "Outside, the storms of war may blow and the lands may be lashed with the fury of its gales, but in our own hearts this Sunday morning there is peace. . . . Our consciences are at rest."

Our consciences as Americans—and as mothers and fathers to our children—will only rest when we demonstrate the leadership and invest the resources to counter the fury the terrorists seek to bring upon us.

Protecting the American people in an age of terrorism demands strong leadership and enormous resources—and it demands them now.

American Water Works Association's National Water Security Conference[5]

Christine Todd Whitman

Administrator, U.S. Environmental Protection Agency (EPA), 2001–03; born New York City, September 26, 1946; grew up in Hunterdon, NJ; B.A. in government, Wheaton College, 1968; outreach worker, Republican National Committee; staff member, U.S. Office of Economic Opportunity; English-as-a-second-language teacher, New York City; Somerset County Board of Chosen Freeholders (county commissioners), 1982–88; New Jersey Board of Public Utilities, 1988–89; Republican candidate for U.S. Senate, 1990; governor of New Jersey, 1993–2001.

Editors' introduction: After the September 11, 2001, terrorist attacks on the United States, many government agencies began revising their policies and practices to prevent further assaults on the nation's facilities, utilities, and citizenry. Former Governor Whitman, who served an abbreviated term as administrator of the Environmental Protection Agency, informed delegates to the American Water Works Association's conference on National Water Security that, "With the onset of war in Iraq, and the heightened state of security here at home, keeping America's water infrastructure safe from attack is . . . a national security imperative." Founded in 1881, the American Water Works Association is an international non-profit scientific and educational society dedicated to the improvement of drinking water quality and supply.

Christine Todd Whitman's speech: Thank you, Jack (Hoffbuhr), for that introduction. I'm pleased to be with you today.

This conference could not be more timely. With the onset of war in Iraq, and the heightened state of security here at home, keeping America's water infrastructure safe from attack is not just a question of environmental security, it's a national security imperative as well.

I am pleased to report that the nation's water sector has done an admirable job responding to the new challenges we have faced since September 11th. Last September, on the first anniversary of the attacks on our country, the *Washington Post* graded the various

---

5. Delivered on March 25, 2003, at Los Angeles, CA.

parts of the nation's critical infrastructure on their response to the new demands they face. The water sector earned a solid "B," one of the highest grades they awarded any sector.

And while I'm not one who believes everything I read in the newspaper, in this case they got it almost exactly right. From everything we've seen, you and your colleagues have taken seriously

EPA's commitment to water security predated September 11th.

your responsibility to protect your facilities from terrorism. The only difference is I would have given you at least a B-plus.

We have been pleased to be able to support your efforts, both with funds, with advice, and with expertise. The work we have done together can be a model for other critical infrastructure sectors.

Of course, EPA's commitment to water security predated September 11th. As a result of Presidential Decision Directives signed in the late nineties, we had begun working with you and others in your industry to evaluate preventive and protective measures that could and should be taken against the possibility of terrorist attacks on the nation's water infrastructure.

Immediately following 9/11, I directed that these various efforts be accelerated. I also created a Water Protection Task Force in the Office of Water to coordinate our efforts in this important area. Due to a great deal of hard work and effort, we were able to complete, months ahead of schedule, the development of a vulnerability assessment methodology for water utilities. We were then able to initiate training for operators in the use of the methodology. We also were able to bring the water ISAC (Information Sharing and Analysis Center) on-line months earlier than scheduled.

In addition, the Water Protection Task Force—which has been ably led by Janet Pawlukiewicz—has completed several important documents that have helped define our work and advance yours. Last year, they completed a comprehensive *State of the Knowledge* assessment, which has been an invaluable tool for guiding our research efforts. They also created and disseminated to utilities the *Baseline Threat Information for Vulnerability Assessments of Community Water Systems*, which is helping you and your counterparts as you undertake your security work.

On top of all that, thanks to a supplemental appropriation from Congress, $90 million was made available to the agency to support the development of vulnerability assessments and security enhancements at thousands of individual utilities. We broke all records in getting money out the door to those who needed it. We disbursed in excess of $50 million to more than 400 of the nation's largest utilities in just a few short months.

Working with states and technical assistance providers, we also dedicated more than $20 million to support similar efforts at medium and small-sized utilities. Ensuring that these utilities receive the support they need is a real priority for me. We must make certain their needs are not overshadowed by those of the nation's largest systems.

Our assigned role as the lead federal agency for the protection of the nation's water infrastructure was expanded with the enactment of the Public Health Security and Bioterrorism Preparedness Response Act this past June.

Under this new law, every public drinking water utility that serves 3,300 or more people—that's nearly 9,000 utilities—is required to conduct a vulnerability assessment. They then must revise their existing emergency response plans within 6 months of completing the vulnerability assessment.

The largest utilities are to have completed their assessments and submitted them to EPA no later than the end of this month. We have already received more than one hundred assessments.

I want to allay any concern some may have about the agency's ability to handle these assessments in a secure fashion. We have established a rigorous set of protocols to ensure that the vulnerability assessments we receive are invulnerable to release. We are treating these assessments as rigorously as we would treat classified information. They are stored in secure safes in a secure location. We are limiting access to those who hold a current, secret-level security clearance. They will remain secure.

All of the work we are doing has been the result of true partnerships. Working together with state and local governments, and with you, I believe we have made tremendous progress toward our shared goal of reducing the vulnerability of our water infrastructure to attack. And the fact of the matter is you are the ones who are doing most of the work. With 165,000 public water utilities, and 16,000 public wastewater utilities in America, there is simply no way the federal government can get this job done alone.

We have relied very heavily on you and other trade organizations to advance our goals. Here at AWWA, your development of training materials, the support you've given to vulnerability assessment training efforts, and conferences such as this, have helped immeasurably in bringing utility operators quickly up to speed on the security challenges we all face.

Your own Research Foundation has been very helpful in identifying and addressing a long list of security-related research and information needs. In fact, it seems to have at least as many projects under way as does EPA in this area.

I should also mention the work done by the Association of Metropolitan Water Agencies. As the private sector lead, AMWA was enormously helpful in getting the ISAC up and running as quickly as possible. The ISAC is the federal government's primary tool for getting homeland security information out to members of the water sector. Last week after the threat was raised to Orange, we used the ISAC to make important and timely information available to water utilities.

Just recently, one of the new senior officials in the Department of Homeland Security pointed to the water ISAC as one of the best among all the critical infrastructure sectors. If your company has not already subscribed to the water ISAC, I urge you to do so.

I have also had the opportunity to visit several water facilities around the country. I've been enormously impressed both with the level of commitment and with the efforts that are under way. From the use of such simple steps as increased vigilance to some cutting-edge technological efforts, America's water sector is meeting its responsibility to the people it serves and to the nation.

As we look to the future, there's no doubt we will be doing more to assist you in meeting that responsibility. One of the three areas our new EPA Homeland Security Research Center is focusing on is detection and treatment of chemical and biological contaminants in water supplies. Our scientists and researchers are very interested in improving that capacity, both at the treatment stage and downstream. I hope this work will not only help advance our security goals, but our clean and safe water goals as well.

In addition, we are looking to build partnerships with other nations that have a wealth of experience in meeting the challenges we have only recently faced. We have, for example, begun to establish a mechanism for sharing information and conducting joint research with water security experts in Israel. Israel has decades of experience in this area, and we hope to be able to utilize that here in the United States.

The most important focus, however, of all our future efforts is you and your counterparts around the nation. The need to protect our water infrastructure against attack is going to be with us for a long time. We look forward to continuing to support you in any way we can in meeting our shared goal of ensuring the safety and security of America's water supply.

Thank you.

Remarks at Department of Homeland Security Employees Event[6]

Tom Ridge

Secretary, Department of Homeland Security, 2003– ; born in Pittsburgh's Steel Valley, August 26, 1945; raised in Erie, PA; B.A. with honors, Harvard University, 1967; infantry staff sargent, U.S. Army, 1968–70, earning the Bronze Star for Valor in Vietnam; J.D., Dickinson School of Law, 1972; private practice 1972–79; assistant district attorney, Erie County, PA, 1979–82; U.S. Congress, 1983–94; governor of Pennsylvania, 1995–2001; Office of Homeland Security adviser, 2001–03.

Editors' introduction: Nearly a month after terrorist hijackers killed thousands of Americans and citizens of some 80 other countries in New York, Washington, D.C., and Pennsylvania on September 11, 2001, President Bush created the White House Office of Homeland Security. On January 24, 2003, the president elevated that office to cabinet status and appointed former governor of Pennsylvania Tom Ridge to be secretary of the newly created Department of Homeland Security. President Bush stated that Secretary Ridge would lead 170,000 "dedicated . . . professionals" in "protecting their fellow Americans." The secretary explained to some of those employees that their "mission" was "to prevent terrorist attacks, reduce our vulnerability to an attack, and minimize loss of life and destruction should another attack occur on American soil."

Tom Ridge's speech: I want to thank the Selfridge Air National Guard for allowing us the use of their base today. I might add that we will never forget the contributions made since 9/11 by members of the army and Air National Guard to make our nation more secure and better prepared.

I want to also thank the vice commandant of the United States Coast Guard, Vice Admiral Thomas J. Barrett, as well as Ninth District Commander Rear Admiral Ronald Silva for attending.

Thank you all for coming today, and for taking a break from your sometimes—most of the time?—stressful jobs.

---

6. Delivered on June 19, 2003, at Selfridge, MI.

You all should be proud of your work. And now you will be able to wear that pride. Each of you has received a pin with the new Department of Homeland Security seal on it. Within the next few weeks, all 180,000-plus of the department's employees will get one.

The American people today are more secure and better prepared than ever before.

You'll notice that the seal features a shield with the three elements you work to protect: our land, sea, and air. It also shows 22 stars, representing the 22 agencies from which you hailed, where many of you were protecting the homeland long before the department came into existence.

Today, however, we're all on the same team—one team, one fight, and one primary mission: to prevent terrorist attacks, reduce our vulnerability to an attack, and minimize loss of life and destruction should another attack occur on American soil.

As the president reminded us Tuesday, we are a nation at war. It is not a war we chose, but it is a war we will win. And until that day, as your pin card says, "We will answer history's call to protect America and preserve our way of life."

Despite our best efforts, despite the work we've done together to start up this new department, we cannot promise that the terrorists will not succeed someday in the future.

But we can say this: that the American people today are more secure and better prepared than ever before.

We are more aware of the threat, and more vigilant about confronting it.

We share more information with the people who need it, including intelligence and law enforcement, our state and local partners, and the private sector.

And we have devoted an unprecedented amount of resources, equipment, and training to our "first preventers" and "first responders" across the land, who protect our hometowns by land, sea, and air.

To date, we've made more than 4 billion dollars available to states and cities to fight terrorism.

That includes more than $42,000,000 to the State of Michigan, funds which can be used for planning, training, equipment, and exercises. Some of the checks have already arrived. And if Congress passes the president's 2004 budget, another $4 billion will be forthcoming—for a total of $8 billion in state and local funding by the end of this year.

This additional funding will help get you the tools you need to detect, protect, and prepare. But put terrorism aside for a moment. Every day, these tools help us become a stronger, more healthy and safer nation—shielded against crime, drug smuggling, natural disasters, and disease.

Let's look at a typical day in homeland security:

On our waterways, you'll find the United States Coast Guard answering, on average, 192 distress calls, performing 109 search and rescue cases, and saving 10 lives. And, I might add, teaching 500 boating safety courses, which may prevent some of the distress calls!

On a typical day you'll see the Coast Guard patrol 90 port security zones, aided by their new Defender Class Response Boats—protecting not just the ports but nearby critical infrastructure such as chemical plants, refineries, and bridges—the American way of life in microcosm.

At our airports, seaports, and border crossings, our agents and inspectors—hundreds more than before 9/11—will process more than 1 million passengers, arriving in 323,000 vehicles, 580 vessels, and 2,400 aircraft.

They will inspect 57,000 trucks and containers, using state-of-the-art scanners and detectors provided by this year's budget—not to mention 1,200 dog teams, which technology can never replace!

They will seize nearly 5,000 pounds of narcotics, nearly half a million dollars in illegal merchandise, and more than $700,000 in illegal currency on a typical day.

And they will apprehend more than 2,600 people trying to cross illegally into the United States. That number has gone down this year, perhaps because our improved security is sending the right message.

On a typical day, our TSA employees will screen about 1.5 million passengers before they board their aircraft.

And they will offer countless smiles to harried travelers, who have responded to these new security measures for the most part with patience and good cheer.

This is a day in the life of homeland security. It makes for a very bad day for criminals and smugglers, not to mention terrorists. And it makes all Americans very proud of the job you do—and thankful that there are so many dedicated Americans willing to do it.

The department's employees perform other duties not directly related to the terrorist threat, but are no less important to this nation.

For instance, we'll provide 1,000 students and school administrators with information on how to survive a tornado. We'll help communities save $2.7 million in damage through flood plain management. And we'll help more than 200 Americans recover from disasters through low-interest loans, insurance, and temporary housing.

Finally, we will naturalize, on average, 1,900 new citizens—people drawn by the American way of life that you and I work so hard to protect.

That way of life is based on the individual—individuals with the freedom to make the right choices.

At the end of the day, that's what homeland security comes down to as well. Individuals free to make decisions but held accountable for them.

Individuals acting on training and instinct—but who need information and innovations from us.

The men and women of homeland security must make billions of decisions a year in order to keep terrorists from being successful even one time. We may use the latest science and technology in that effort—but they are our most valuable resource.

Diana Dean is one of them. In December 1999, U.S. Customs inspector Dean stopped a driver coming into the U.S. from Canada. He was driving the last car to come off of the last ferry that arrived that day in Port Angeles, Washington. Acting on her instincts and training, she noticed his suspicious behavior and unusual answers to her questions. She asked the driver to step out of his car and opened his trunk. What she found was the makings of a bomb—the Millennium bomb, as it's become known. Her action saved perhaps hundreds of lives and led to the capture of several Al Qaeda cell members in the U.S.

We will focus the greatest resources on the greatest threats and vulnerabilities, so we can protect our way of life.

At the end of a long and tiring day, her instincts were still sharp, and a terrible act was prevented.

Diana is a true American hero—but she'll probably tell you she was just doing her job. Diana now works, like you, for the Department of Homeland Security—and we're proud that she continues to "just do her job" for us.

It's proof that one person can make a difference. And 180,000 people with a variety of skills, working behind one primary mission, can make a huge difference.

The Department of Homeland Security will get you the tools and training you need to build new barriers to terrorists—and build new bridges to our many partners—the states and localities, business and industry, scientific community, schools and universities, and foreign governments, who are helping us catch terrorists, seize their funds, and identify high-risk cargo long before they reach American shores.

We will put the right infrastructure in place to create a culture of excellence and weave a fabric of protection to make all Americans safer.

And we will focus the greatest resources on the greatest threats and vulnerabilities, so we can protect our way of life as well—as we're doing with Canada right now, working to create "smart borders" that keep terrorists out but do not stem the flow of commerce or legitimate travel.

It all adds up to a department that is "ready, not waiting," and certainly not afraid.

One of our first challenges, as you know, is to build a model human resources system. We take this very seriously.

Today's event is part of a nine-city regional town hall meeting tour for employees and their representatives. We will sit down with employees and listen to your needs so we can present a full range of options to the Senior Review Committee later this year for recommendations.

I have no doubt you will give us great ideas—and that together, we will meet this challenge.

I want to conclude by offering a little of my perspective. As secretary of the department, I am privileged to witness the hard work you do and the value you bring to this department. But I also get to see the impression you make on the American people.

You have shown them that one person—and one department—can make a real difference.

And that is making it a lot easier for me to convince Americans to take that one extra step—to join Citizen Corps or a CERTS team, or invest a little more on security for their small business, or report suspicious activity to the proper authorities—or simply to log on to Ready.gov and teach their family the best way to survive an attack. And at the end of the day, that's what it's all about.

The other day I visited Boston to issue port security grants and talk about our many port security initiatives. While there I toured Boston Harbor in a new police interceptor boat we helped fund.

I was moved to learn that when the factory workers making the engine heard the boat was for homeland security, they pulled it off the line and made special improvements to it.

Everyone, it seemed, wanted to do their part to secure the homeland. They went that extra mile—because they see all of you going the extra mile, every single day.

So once again, thank you for inspiring not just vigilance, but confidence from the American people in our shared ability to meet the threat. Thank you.

III. Freedom of Speech

Academic Freedom Award[1]

Mark R. Hamilton

President, University of Alaska System, 1998– ; born February 25, 1945; B.S., U.S. Military Academy at West Point, 1967; M.A. in English literature, Florida State University, 1972; graduated Armed Forces Staff College in Virginia, 1976; graduated U.S. Army War College in Pennsylvania, 1986; U.S. Army, retiring as major general, 1967–98; commander for U.S. military group in El Salvador, helping to negotiate (in Spanish) an end to 12-year civil war in that country, 1990–92; Distinguished Service Medal, U.S. Army, 1992; Joint Distinguished Service Medal, Armed Forces, 1997.

Editors' introduction: After the terrorist attacks on the United States on September 11, 2001, civil and other leaders joined a continuing dialogue concerning how best to protect the nation from further assaults, while others debated what should and should not be said about homeland security. Some insisted that people should be cautious in their criticisms and claims, while others reminded that freedom of expression is one of the hallmarks of the democratic society that Americans value and defend. President Hamilton expressed concern about "attempted curtailments" of free speech "in our nation's universities," where "academic freedom" is "central to the expanding of knowledge." The National Association of Scholars, which gave Hamilton the Academic Freedom Award, is an organization of professors, graduate students, college administrators and trustees, and independent scholars committed to rational discourse as the foundation of academic life in a free and democratic society.

Mark R. Hamilton's speech: I am, of course, greatly honored by this award. I am as well perplexed that a simple assertion of the right to freedom of speech can be seen as extraordinary.

This is especially enigmatic when we consider that, according to a 2001 poll conducted by the Center for Research and Analysis at the University of Connecticut, "fully 93 percent of Americans continue to support the right of fellow citizens to express unpopular opinions."

My own explanation of this enigma—that is, that something supported by 93 percent of Americans can be newsworthy—is that we observe a somewhat different data point. That is, that almost 100

---

1. Delivered on March 10, 2002, at the Princess Hotel, Fairbanks, AK. Reprinted with permission of Mark R. Hamilton.

percent of Americans believe in the freedom to express unpopular opinions 93 percent of the time. The other 7 percent falling into the category of "Oh, *that* unpopular opinion."

Internationally, the abridgement of First Amendment rights may come from a liberal interpretation of the caveat in our own Constitution: that is, "clear and present danger."

The claim of such a threshold breech, at least at the national level, is hardly contrivable in America. It is more considerable in countries with long histories of revolution and governmental ouster. Advocating the overthrow of government through speech, press, peaceable assemblage, and petition may be seen as a greater threat in countries where the incumbents came to power by the same devices. Still, it is a very slippery slope that more often than not ignores the distinction between "clear and present danger" to the nation and "clear and present danger" to the unchallenged authority of the incumbent regime.

> *I am greatly concerned by the nearly ubiquitous examples of inappropriate curtailments or retributions for the practice of free speech.*

Sadly, domestically, we seem to have gone beyond the stretching of the existing constitutional litmus test and have simply replaced it with a threshold so amorphous and convenient as to constitute no threshold at all. There is so little substance to observed current practice that descriptions are difficult. A few of the forms of exclusion from free speech protections that seem most common suggest something like, "alleged and possible insult," "demonstrated political incorrectness," or the more recent, "insufficient patriotism." Somehow the First Amendment offers less assurance when we assert, "these rights shall not be abridged except in the case of alleged and possible insult," or in the case of "demonstrated political incorrectness," and so forth.

I am greatly concerned by the nearly ubiquitous examples of inappropriate curtailments or retributions for the practice of free speech. I am especially concerned to observe attempted curtailments in our nation's universities. Here freedom of speech is essential to academic freedom, and academic freedom central to the expanding of knowledge. Academic freedom is central to the whole concept of the dialectic where thesis meets antithesis, is debated, leads to synthesis more closely approximating truth. This synthesis takes its role as the new thesis, again to be confronted in the contest of ideas leading us farther forward in our understanding.

Where freedom of speech is threatened, we will find a distinct lack of antithesis—a lack of challenge to the prevailing wisdom, condemning us to wander in a shadow world of "right thinking" and sameness. It is only somewhat comforting that truth cannot forever be repressed. It is a rare individual who will step forward in an atmosphere of controlled thought. There are as few Martin Luthers as there are Martin Luther King, Jr.s.

In that world of shadow, debate gives way to what are tantamount to rallies for a cause. I am reminded of an unlikely recognition of this phenomenon. Unlikely in the case of the observer and of the site of observation. At the height of the Vietnam conflict, the famous playwright Arthur Miller was invited to speak at the United States Military Academy at West Point. He was actually invited twice after it was learned that he thought the first invitation to be a bad joke. He was reluctant, but with the same resolution that had sustained his early and passionate denunciation of that war, he went to West Point and presented his lecture. In the ensuing discussions, he was shocked to hear the voices of decorated veterans of Vietnam support his views and add to them. He was not so surprised to hear other voices challenging and even ridiculing his stance. Nonetheless, after the trip he wrote an article in which he remarked on the irony he had witnessed. After dozens of speeches on dozens of campuses, he reported that the only campus in America where the Vietnam War was seriously being debated was at West Point.

Faculty-led rallies are fine, but they ought not be confused with serious intellectual debate. We don't need debate or the dialectic if our objective is rote recitation. We need them desperately if our objective is learning and learning to learn.

What is at stake is not trivial. Earl Warren, former U.S. chief justice said this: "Teachers and students must always remain free to inquire, to study and to evaluate, to gain new maturity and understanding; otherwise our civilization will stagnate and die."

Questions with one answer are catechisms (and perhaps some special cases of lower-level mathematics).

Being an outsider to the world of universities, I was surprised to discover the alleged nexus of tenure to academic freedom.

Let me pause a moment to make an important clarification because I now have the attention of every academic in the audience. Between books I bought myself and those sent to me by friends, I must have read a dozen books by former university presidents about the job I had undertaken. These were less valuable than one might hope and a bit perplexing as I noted that apparently what one does upon retirement is to write a book trashing the profession that has nurtured one's life work. In any case, the dozen books had two consistent themes: You're going to have trouble with your education department, and tenure is the great Satan.

Frankly, I don't get it. It seems to me that tenure is a useful and important investment on the part of the institution to recognize, reward, and retain the best of our faculty. It is certainly true that tenure will always be difficult to explain to audiences outside of the academy, but equally true that we make precious little effort to try to explain.

What yet fails me is the direct association of tenure with freedoms of speech and publication and petition. One need not work for seven years to earn a right to freedoms guaranteed at birth. Additionally, tenure is overwhelmingly described in terms of protections from externally imposed restrictions, from politicians or administrators. Yet that same faculty counsel will, almost to the person, relate tales of significant direct and implied threats to the gaining of tenure status from within their current or previous department or school.

My survey is neither scientific nor extensive, dozens of tenured faculty members not thousands. Still, I would offer advice to those who would pursue this thought more rigorously. Don't ask the theoretical, "Do you think that there are significant pressures within your department to conform, or be silent, or to be deferential in your expressed ideas in order to earn tenure." The answer to that question will be almost certainly, "no." Ask instead, "Have you ever experienced significant pressures, etc." Here the answer will be overwhelmingly "yes." The differences in the answers are less dramatic if you are talking to a professor who has not yet earned tenure.

If such pressures exist to the point that I believe they do, the salt in the wound is that such an atmosphere will not be resolved by tenure. Instead, the next leverage point will be the promotion to full professor, and following that the competition for a chair.

I am reminded of one of the first recorded cases of bait and switch. After seven years of indentured servitude in the seeking of Rachel's hand in marriage, Jacob is given Leah, and the chance to work seven years more for the prize he sought.

To be more secular, in an admittedly unkind assessment of U.S. foreign policy in the early '90s, I noted that we seemed dedicated to the classic carrot and stick approach to diplomacy. Unfortunately we chose to beat our allies with the carrot and make them eat the stick.

Freedom of speech is the mechanism for diversity of thought. That is beyond diversity in the current usage of the term. If we are not ensuring diversity of thought all of our efforts to pursue ethnic and gender and all the other diversities are only important first steps, not sufficiency. Without diversity of thought we are creating little more than decoupage. Most departments are eager to welcome to their midst professors of different race or creed or gender; far fewer are eager to welcome to their midst professors whose view of history or of economics or of philosophy or politics and so forth differ markedly from the department norm. That is the diversity we ought to offer to our students and to one another.

I will close with one more thought.

There are many in this room that have studied this topic more deeply and more intellectually than I have. I acknowledge that as I offer my own pedestrian view of how we got to this point.

I will use a couple of sweeping generalizations to press a few important points, and offer a bit of hope. Point one is that attempts to modify the practice of freedom of speech originate in all aspects of the political spectrum, and so its defense must be embraced by a similar broad-based political will. Point two is that we are at an important point of intervention at this exact moment in history.

Sweeping generalizations follow: My lifetime has observed two nearly equal periods of struggle over the modification of First Amendment rights. For the first 25 or so years the reluctance to support unqualified practice of these rights was most evident from the right of the political spectrum with the organized defense of free speech and other First Amendment rights represented by the left of the political spectrum. In the last 25 years or so these roles have been nearly completely reversed. I would observe that the role change was more quickly and completely embraced by the modifiers than it was by the defenders.

Most recently in the pathos extending from Sept 11th, more conservative voices have begun to express outrage at the expression of any opinion deemed not sufficiently patriotic. Is this the start of 25 years of political correctness choreographed by the right of the political spectrum? Will there be a whole new series of penalty boxes for the unenlightened? Will mandatory sensitivity training be replaced with mandatory flag saluting? Who will be the new self-anointed guardians of right thinking? With John Wayne dead and Charlton Heston getting old, how will we gather sufficient movie stars to tell us which trees to cut, which animals to lift protection from?

I don't want a new cast of mind police.

I didn't like it when the political right stifled diversity of thought.

I didn't like when the political left stifled diversity of thought.

I used to think the greatest warning phrase one could hear was "with all due respect . . . ," because I knew something ugly was going to follow. I now cringe most when I hear or read the phrase, "We believe in freedom of speech, but . . . ."

What will follow that "but" will be a limiting of free speech on other than constitutionally guaranteed grounds. It should be rejected.

Lack of political correctness is not clear and present danger.

Possible insult is not clear and present danger.

Insufficient patriotism is not clear and present danger.

Congress shall make no law abridging the freedom of speech.

Let's follow suit.

The State of Freedom Post 9/11[2]

Paul K. McMasters

First Amendment ombudsman, Freedom Forum's First Amendment Center, Arlington, VA, 1995– ; born Dade County, MO, January 18, 1942; B.A. (1965) and M.A. (1973) in English, Southwest Missouri State University; U.S. Army, retiring as captain, 1965–70; managing editor, the Kansas Coffeyville Journal, *1979–82;* USA Today, *1982–92, associate editor of its editorial pages, 1991–92; National Freedom of Information chair, Society of Professional Journalists, 1986–90; executive director, Freedom Forum First Amendment Center, Vanderbilt University, 1992–95; president, Society of Professional Journalists (SPJ), 1993–94; president, SDX Foundation, the education arm of SPJ; president, Virginia Coalition for Open Government, 2002– ; has appeared on* Today, NewsHour, Larry King Live, Crossfire, Fox News Channel, *and* Court TV; *Wells Memorial Key, SPJ's highest award for distinguished service to the society, 1990; charter member, Freedom of Information Act Hall of Fame, 1996; John Peter and Anna Catherine Zenger Award for lifetime achievement on behalf of the First Amendment, 2000; authored articles and columns.*

Editors' introduction: After terrorists killed thousands of people in New York, Washington, D.C., and Pennsylvania in 2001, discussions ensued about how to protect American citizens and what constraints, if any, should be imposed upon that dialogue. Freedom of Information Oklahoma, Inc. sponsored the Fourth Annual First Amendment Congress, November 7 and 8, 2002. In addressing that conference, Mr. McMasters outlined "restraints imposed on free speech since 9/11" and called attention to losses of "freedom of expression and freedom of information" in a country whose leaders seem to be "looking over our shoulder." The Freedom Forum First Amendment Center, for which Mr. McMasters is ombudsman, is a nonpartisan foundation dedicated to free press, free speech, and free spirit for all people.

Paul K. McMasters's speech: It has been more than a year since September 11, but its unspeakable terror still holds us in its grip. It has had an indelible impact on the national conscience. Its fears were compounded by the anthrax attack and anxious speculation about biological, nuclear, chemical, agricultural, critical infrastructure, and a host of other threats to our individual and collective

---

2. Delivered on November 7, 2002, in Constitution Hall, University of Central Oklahoma, at Edmond, OK. Reprinted with permission of Paul K. McMasters.

security—including the sniper attacks last month in the nation's capital that transfixed Americans across the land.

The way we have been responding to these new fears brings us face to face with an awful truth: Freedom is very fragile.

> ***There have been numerous restraints imposed on free speech since 9/11.***

I was asked to try to measure for you some of what besides our innocence about terror we have lost because of September 11, 2001.

The loss list is sobering in its length.

For that reason, I'll confine myself to just two categories of concern: freedom of expression and freedom of information [access to government records].

There have been numerous restraints imposed on free speech since 9/11—by our leaders and by ourselves:

- Immediately, the president's chief spokesman warned Americans that they'd better be careful what they said and the media to be careful what they published or broadcast.

- College professors were punished for comments in the classroom.

- Newspaper editors, columnists, and cartoonists were reprimanded or fired by their bosses for their opinions. Too many journalists, I'm afraid, sported American flags on their lapels and TV screens and refrained from sharp questions for fear of appearing unpatriotic or subversive.

- Bill Maher's *Politically Incorrect* TV show was boycotted by advertisers for a comment he made about the attacks.

That, unfortunately, is just a brief sampling.

These sorts of things could be expected, I suppose, in the aftermath of an event of such magnitude. But the restrictions on speech, press, and access soon became much more systemic in policy changes, legislation, and law enforcement actions. And some of them—intentionally or otherwise—went far beyond the war on terrorism.

In the immediate aftermath of 9/11 and the commencement of the war on terrorism, the executive branch put into place a number of policies and actions that impacted on the ability of the American people to gain information that would help it evaluate and support in an informed way the actions and policies of their leaders.

Restrictions on the press:

- Cameras and film were seized at Ground Zero.

- Media aircraft were grounded long after other general aircraft returned to the air.
- The Pentagon bought up exclusive rights to satellite images of the combat region.
- Unprecedented restrictions were placed on journalists covering the war in Afghanistan.
- The White House warned news executives about coverage of Osama bin Laden and the Taliban.

Restrictions on access:

- By executive order, President Bush eviscerated the Presidential Records Act, just as it went into effect.
- Attorney General Ashcroft issued a new FOIA implementation memo that, in effect, turned the presumption of openness on its head.
- The Justice Department denied access to information about more than one thousand detainees rounded up as suspects, material witnesses, or for other reasons after September 11.
- The White House dramatically reduced the number of intelligence briefings for Congress and the number of members who could attend those briefings.
- The White House ignored requests from Congress for information on a wide range of topics, including the vice president's energy task force, the FBI's mob informants, and the decision to relax restrictions on coal-fired plant emissions.
- Hundreds of government Web pages were taken down.

For its part, Congress also acted in ways that surrendered to our fears and put at risk our freedoms. It accepted without much complaint a hastily assembled wish list of proposals from the executive branch. That package became the U.S.A. PATRIOT Act, and it gave our government broad new powers over our lives. Some of these proposals had been around for years but had not been able to make it into law because of congressional reservations about their impact on civil liberties.

Some of the PATRIOT Act's provisions put an indirect but frigid chill on the free-speech rights of American citizens.

Among those provisions rushed into law were expanded powers to tap our phones, paw through our library records, monitor our Web site visits, read our e-mail, scrutinize our religious worship, listen in on attorney-client conversations, and mine private databases for more information about us.

In addition, the Justice Department proposed a citizen informant project in which a million letter carriers, meter readers, cable installers, and others who routinely enter our homes would be trained to spot and report activity they considered suspicious.

There is no measuring of the impact on our First Amendment activities—what we say privately and publicly, what we read, who we talk to, where we worship—when we know someone from the government is looking over our shoulder as we do so.

One does not have to be either paranoid or unpatriotic to be concerned about the ability of government officials to invade nearly every aspect of our First Amendment activities. In many instances, our government could take these actions without any meaningful warrant to do so or instrument of accountability as to what has been done, how often, and to whom. Or without attaching those actions to an actual impact on terrorism in the way of real results.

Legislation to establish the Homeland Security Department promises to aggravate these problems.

One does not have to be either paranoid or unpatriotic to be concerned about the ability of government officials to invade nearly every aspect of our First Amendment activities.

One proposal would blow a huge hole in the Freedom of Information Act. The exemption has been pushed by the technology industry, utilities, financial services firms, manufacturers, and others. It would free businesses from the disclosure requirements of local and state laws—and grant them immunity from civil liability for violations of securities, tax, civil rights, environmental, labor, consumer protection, health, and safety laws that might be revealed in the information they provide.

More importantly, it would deny to the public crucial information about hazardous materials, chemical releases, toxic spills, and other threats to health and safety—not to mention vulnerabilities to terrorism and sabotage. There would be a real risk that critical infrastructure vulnerabilities would be worse if the information about how private businesses are running nuclear and chemical plants, refineries, water systems, and other facilities is hidden from public scrutiny.

In other words, this exemption would not be your ordinary loophole but rather a standing invitation for companies with something to hide to label incriminating material as "critical infrastructure information," submit it to the new department, and thus put it beyond the reach of the public, the press, the Congress, and the courts.

There is a long list of reasons why writing this exemption into the Homeland Security legislation is no way for the government to do business.

First among them is the fact that such an exemption is unnecessary. The FOIA already exempts from disclosure real national security information as well as trade secrets and confidential business information. The courts are consistently deferential to such claims. And administration officials, as well as some in the private sector, concede that the exemption is not necessary.

Certainly, there are secrets that must be kept—information that would indeed harm the U.S. and help its enemies if disclosed. But truly dangerous information already is protected from disclosure.

Without public access to the kind of information that would be exempted in this proposal, businesses, in effect, will have their own Private Sector Security Act that creates an environment where there is no accountability for mistakes and misdeeds, no public pressure to address critical infrastructure vulnerabilities, and no informed discourse on policies that impact dramatically on public life.

That means that critical vulnerabilities would not be identified, the solutions proposed would not be known, and any efforts to fix them would go unchecked.

But that's not all. The Homeland Security legislation also would remove legal protections for government employees who go to our elected leaders or to the press or public to warn of incompetence, errors, or corruption.

How do restrictions on access to government information chill your speech, hamper the press, and ultimately diminish all of our freedoms? And can we demonstrate real improvements in our security to warrant any changes in our freedom?

These are serious questions that should be examined more deliberately than we seem to have done thus far.

There is security in knowledge and information. If national security is government's top priority, then its operations and policies must be as transparent as possible. What an irony it is when our government places a high priority on warning us about the risks of vitamin supplements and the hazards of playground equipment but keeps from us even the most rudimentary information about the vulnerabilities of our highways and waterways, chemical and nuclear plants, and other parts of the nation's critical infrastructure.

Don't we need a broader definition of national security than protecting our shores from invasion and our skyscrapers from attacks? Shouldn't that definition also include the security of the citizenry's basic freedoms? Aren't those very freedoms—the freedom to inquire, to speak, to protest, to participate—aren't they ultimately more important to our security as history's longest-lived democracy than a vast array of antiterrorism measures that sees the solution as protective measures only and not preventive measures also? Is it truly a solution to view citizens as helpless beings who must be protected rather than as partners in the effort to protect us all?

We must keep constantly in mind the even larger dimension to this whole idea of access to government information. Speech is meaningless, a free press is toothless, and the civic conversation mere prattle without access. Without information, Americans cannot engage persuasively in the public discourse that is their right and responsibility.

Then there is the matter of checks and balances. Congress loses its ability to conduct oversight of federal agencies and hold them accountable if it is denied access to even basic information about how the executive branch conducts its affairs in the name of Americans.

St. John's University political scientists Matthew Crenson and Benjamin Ginsburg have just published a book examining a recent development in our democracy: where Americans view themselves and are viewed by their leaders as "customers" of government

---

Speech is meaningless, a free press is toothless, and the civic conversation mere prattle without access.

---

rather than as citizens who form the government. This is a pernicious idea. It masks a threat to the balance of power in our democracy. When government views Americans as customers rather than citizens and the executive branch treats courts and Congress as enablers rather than partners, then suppression and servitude rather than freedom lurk in our future.

We also must ask whether all Americans are paying their fair share in these sacrifices of freedoms.

Certainly not corporate citizens, who are demanding to be relieved of compliance with the FOIA before they will do their part in hardening the nation's critical infrastructure against accident and sabotage and attack.

On the other end, certainly not government workers in the new Homeland Security Department, who will be denied the whistleblower protections accorded their colleagues elsewhere in the government.

Certainly not ordinary Americans, who are being told to allow more government into their own lives and to get by with less information about government policies and decision-making.

We have accepted the idea that Americans should not have access to classified material. But our leaders have attempted to expand that body of information to material that is "classifiable."

Now, they are proposing yet another category of information to be beyond the reach of the public and the press: "sensitive but unclassified."

It is crucial that we accept these developments only after rigorous public debate and only after ascertaining whether they actually will improve our security and be worth the cost.

Why is access so vital?

Because the press must have it in order to facilitate the flow of information among the three branches of government and the citizenry.

Because the Congress must have it in order to provide proper oversight and accountability.

Because the people must have it in order to engage in truly democratic discourse.

Sometimes it's smart to be afraid. Other times, fear makes us downright stupid.

For example, it sometimes makes us stumble into dumb dilemmas, such as saying that we have to choose between security or freedom. We can have both.

Another stupid assertion that stems from fear and panic: We are safer by not knowing than by knowing. We are not necessarily safer in the dark than in the light.

> *It is always smart to examine any policy that threatens to limit our freedoms because it is so hard to get them back after they are gone.*

It is always smart to examine any policy that threatens to limit our freedoms because it is so hard to get them back after they are gone. There is plenty of evidence that we have not sufficiently examined some of the actions and proposed actions that have been taken in the name of more security—and less freedom—in the wake of 9/11.

More and more the streams of information flowing to the public are choked off. We demand more secrecy for security. We give up access for disclosure. We privatize government data for revenue. We restrict access to electronic court records for privacy.

What an irony. In the Information Age, when we imagine we are awash in information, overwhelmed by it, struggling to find ways to manage it, it is difficult to make the case for the idea that we are being systematically deprived of it. We have a hard time admitting that we are receiving less and less information with which to protect ourselves and our national security.

When faced with such threats as we are today, we are much more willing to yield up some of our freedoms. While that impulse is understandable, it is a bargain with the devil. Benjamin Franklin spoke of this dilemma more than two centuries ago when he said, "They that can give up essential liberty to obtain a little temporary safety deserve neither liberty nor safety."

We nod in agreement when we hear those words, but we lack the will to follow them to their necessary result.

It is our right *as individuals*, of course, to relinquish whatever freedoms we want whenever we want. But it is the constitutional guarantors of freedom—such as the First Amendment—that we are not free to give away, no matter how daunting the crisis we face. When we do that, we not only rob our fellow citizens of their freedoms, we run the real risk of sentencing our grandchildren to a life much less than what it should be. Certainly, we do not bequeath them the democracy that we were handed to protect.

I think we need to confront the contradiction between the executive branch's new formula for security: information-sharing. It wants government agencies to share more information with one another. It wants the branches of government to share more information with one another. It wants other nations to share more information with it. It wants corporations to share more information with the government. It wants private citizens to share information.

But it insists that the government must share less information with everyone else.

For citizens of a democracy to accept that without challenge is to forget the bitter lessons of 9/11. It was, after all, the failure to share information that contributed to our tragic vulnerability.

The failure of agencies to share with one another and with congressional oversight committees.

The failure of the committees to share with the press.

The failure of the press to ask the right questions and hold public officials accountable.

And the failure of an informed public to hold all of them accountable by demanding—and heeding—information about our vulnerabilities.

So, we are reduced to this brief characterization about the state of freedom in the United States after September 11:

When the fundamental components of a free and open society—freedom of speech, freedom of the press, and access to government information—are so readily and easily dismissed in the face of fear, then there is no doubt that our freedoms are fragile indeed and that none of our freedoms are secure when these fundamental freedoms are on such uncertain footing.

Thank you.

Principles of Speech and Expression[3]

John J. DeGioia

President, Georgetown University, 2001– ; born Waco, TX, January 16, 1957; B.A. in English, 1979, and Ph.D. in philosophy, Georgetown University, 1995; at Georgetown University: professorial lecturer and faculty member, Department of Philosophy; assistant to president, 1982–85; dean of student affairs, 1985–1992; associate vice president and chief administrative officer for the main campus, 1992–95; vice president, 1995–98; senior vice president, 1998–2001; board of directors, Washington Foundation for Psychiatry; participant in the Forum for the Future of Higher Education; Georgetown Alumni Admissions Program Chairman's Award, 1997.

Editors' introduction: When President DeGioia addressed some 70 students, administrators, and faculty attending the Student Speech and Expression Forum at Georgetown University, the Bush administration appeared to be preparing the nation for war in Iraq. In this tense atmosphere, some supported the administration's position that President Saddam Hussein's Iraqi regime possessed weapons of mass destruction that threatened the world, while others insisted that claim did not justify going to war. Advocates also disagreed concerning whether citizens should openly criticize a nation preparing for war. In this setting, President DeGioia advised that, "while free speech will cause pain . . . we truly believe, by permitting the broadest range of discourse—some of it unpopular, some of it disturbing—that truth will emerge."

John J. DeGioia's speech: Let me begin this forum by arguing two different points of view regarding free speech and expression. This tension has shaped our discourse here, and I hope to do it justice.

The first point of view: Georgetown should curtail speech *because* we believe strongly that ideas matter. Ideas are conveyed in speech, and ideas can be very dangerous. They can upset the status quo; they can be disruptive. Ideas can generate negative reactions, carry hate, wound people, and cause real trauma.

Ideas are powerful. College students are at a formative time in their lives; they are easily persuaded; they may not grasp the complexity of some ideas. If you believe in the power of ideas, then you

---

3. Delivered on February 3, 2003, in McNeir Auditorium, Washington, D.C. Reprinted with permission of John J. DeGioia.

must consider carefully what ideas are promulgated at George-town. Specifically, one must consider that a campus committed to unrestricted speech could, on occasion, appear to provide a legiti-mate platform for lies, hatred, distortion, and error. As a result, offensive speech appears to acquire legitimacy when it occurs on the grounds of a respected research institution or is uttered by members of that community.

Active debate and discussion of ideas are, in fact, the signs of a healthy intellectual community.

Now let's consider a second viewpoint—that a university should commit itself to free speech and expression.

Universities are predicated on a fundamental trust that permits the broadest possible intellectual freedom and autonomy. Univer-sities are also committed to the idea that the truth is achieved in dialogue. To limit dialogue a priori is to show a lack of confidence in the capacity of the individual to discover truth. The university is a catalyst and container of conflict; and there will be conflict. Active debate and discussion of ideas are, in fact, the signs of a healthy intellectual community.

Two points of view. Both matter. Good arguments can be made for both.

The question of what constitutes the appropriate range of speech and expression raises the most difficult and important issues for the academy. We live this tension as a community. At George-town, our decision has been to create a framework that supports open fora and free expression.

This evening, I'd like to talk about why we made the choice to support and protect free and open speech, the pain it sometimes causes, the obligations it places on all of us, and finally, why we believe this approach works best in an academic community.

Georgetown has chosen to permit the widest possible discourse, limited only under certain exceptional circumstances, because we believe in three things: the value of intellectual inquiry, the integ-rity of individuals, and the ability of members of this university community to think rationally about ideas and work toward truth. We cannot be a university dedicated to intellectual excellence and at the same time place limits on what might be said and thought and discussed.

Our policy on free speech and expression was developed at Geor-getown 14 years ago to provide a framework for our common life together. It does not prohibit speech based on the person present-ing ideas or the content of those ideas nor does it mandate any mechanism by which the institution decides who gets to speak and who doesn't. We don't approve or endorse the speakers that come here. That's known and widely understood.

At the same time, we understand that free speech will cause pain. Open debate can be difficult and uncomfortable. Our trust will, on occasion, be abused. William Shockley, a Nobel laureate, was invited to speak on many campuses in the 1960s, despite the fact that he used his stature in the scientific world to make outrageous claims about racial inferiority.

There can be a tragic element in any pursuit of truthfulness. We can't ignore the tragic dimension of our lives, but we truly believe, by permitting the broadest range of discourse—some of it unpopular, some of it disturbing—that truth will emerge.

Our commitment to free speech carries with it the obligation to engage difficult, even offensive, ideas. In the context of that obligation, Georgetown has taken many risks. Many of you know of the tragic murder of Archbishop Oscar Romero, the Salvadoran priest who received an honorary degree from Georgetown in 1978 for his courageous advocacy for the poor. Two years later, Archbishop Romero was murdered, apparently by paramilitary forces aligned with the Salvadoran government. Some years later, Roberto D'Aubuisson, one who many felt was responsible for that murder, was hosted at Georgetown. His appearance triggered uncomfortable, emotional debate. D'Aubuisson had his say and so did his opponents.

> *Our commitment to free speech carries with it the obligation to engage difficult, even offensive, ideas.*

More recently, a controversial author, Norman Finkelstein, was hosted on this campus in November, stirring up hurt feelings and fury. In the tradition of Cardinal Newman, who held that the best response to a controversial speech is *more* speech, not censorship, those angered by Finkelstein's presence on campus gathered in Red Square to make their views known.

If you can't debate controversial ideas here, where can it be done? This is the unique role and responsibility of the academy. It is a role we must play if we are to sustain a civil society. The writer Ron Suskind once told me that the university is the last place where there is still "untitled land" in the public square. Every other piece of ground has been claimed in support of some particular interest.

Our obligation to protect open fora carries a cost that is and will continue to be borne by everyone in this audience—consider the outrage of some Jesuits after D'Aubuisson spoke here; or the outrage of some members of the Jewish community and some supporters of Palestine after certain speakers have spoken here, or the outrage of pro-life supporters after appearances by abortion rights supporters. And many members of this community are outraged when Catholic leaders invited here express support for the death penalty in a way that runs counter to the position of the Church.

In fact, some argue that sustaining an open forum conflicts with our Catholic and Jesuit tradition. I disagree for three reasons:

First, Catholicism respects the dignity of the individual learner and places great weight on the power and importance of conscience.

Second, we find in Catholic intellectual tradition numerous examples of Catholic thought leaders exploring controversial ideas and over time coming to discover God's wisdom more accurately.

And finally, because this is a Catholic institution, we are not neutral in the marketplace of ideas and thus invite speakers whose views we think you ought to consider.

In this role, I invited Avery Cardinal Dulles to campus in November, and this semester invited J. Bryan Hehir, president of Catholic Charities USA. I felt it was essential for the ideas of Cardinal Dulles and Fr. Hehir to be part of campus discourse. I also invited Michael Walzer to talk about Jewish values and universalism. It is critically important that our community understand Jewish civilization and intellectual life. Dr. Walzer enriched our community immensely.

We will defend the ability of members of this academic community to invite speakers you deem to be important, but I also want you to consider that you also have an obligation to consider the implications of some invitations. This is your community, built and nourished by generations before you, and I ask you to demonstrate respect in the nature of speakers you invite. I also ask you to respect the opinions of those who would disagree with someone you invite and when possible, to structure events to provide an opportunity for dialogue that includes a variety of viewpoints.

When you find it necessary to respond to speech you find offensive or inappropriate, I ask you to respect the principle of the open fora and the needs of others to express ideas. By all means make your views known with counter argument and with dignified protests. By all means, attend the lecture and ask the speaker to defend the views in question. Be thoughtful in how you express yourself. And please do not take it upon yourself to attempt to silence a speaker, to shout someone down, to discard publications, or to destroy signs that announce a speaker's appearance. Such actions are not in keeping with our tradition, and it is not the kind of speech that we protect. As always in approaching a great and complex idea like free speech and expression, St. Ignatius offers wisdom. In his writings, he calls on us "to be more eager to put a good interpretation on a neighbor's statement than to condemn it." What does that mean? Ignatius is asking us to listen thoughtfully, to be charitable in our views, and to recognize that intellectual breakthrough requires our openness to ideas that are unfamiliar.

Finally, why do we believe that a policy of free speech and expression, with its inevitable pain and its attendant obligations, is the right approach? What do we hope will emerge? We would like each person to thoughtfully consider opposing points of view, to dwell in uncertainty and maybe even to be comfortable there. My early studies as an English major lead me down a road with John Keats to a concept called negative capability, a difficult idea perhaps captured best by Walter Jackson Bate in his biography of Keats.

Bate wrote: "In our life of uncertainties, where no one system or formula can explain everything, what is needed is an imaginative openness of mind and a heightened receptivity to reality in its full and diverse concreteness. This however involves negating one's ego."

Bruce Springsteen had his own way of saying the same thing: "You've got to be able to hold a lot of contradictory ideas in your mind without going nuts. I feel like to do my job right, when I walk out onstage I've got to feel like it's the most important thing in the world. I've also got to feel like, well, it's only rock and roll."

For myself, I've never regretted putting myself in a position where I've had to consider another point of view. By listening, you better understand an opposing position or see a weakness in an argument that you may not have understood before. I may not change my position, but I've learned something valuable.

At this moment in history, when the nation debates the possibility of war, I would much prefer to be in this community of diverse wisdom, even when there is disagreement and discord—because here young people are challenged to form opinions in matters so important that neutrality is not an option.

I expect we'll all learn something valuable in this forum. In the important tradition of a free and open exchange, I look forward to the ideas of others.

Preserving an Open Democracy in a Time of Crisis[4]

Bob Giles

Curator, Nieman Foundation for Journalism, Harvard University, 2000– ; born Cleveland, OH, June 6, 1933; B.A. in English, DePauw University, 1955; M.S. in journalism, Columbia University, 1956; reporter, managing editor, executive editor, Akron (Ohio) Beacon Journal, *1958–76; Gannett professional-in-residence, William Allen White School of Journalism, University of Kansas, 1976–77; executive editor and editor,* Rochester (New York) Democrat & Chronicle *and* Times-Union, *1977–86; executive editor and editor,* Detroit News, *1986–97; senior vice president, The Freedom Forum, and executive director of its Media Studies Center, 1997–2000, editing* Media Studies Journal; *president, American Society of Newspaper Editors and Associated Press Managing Editors; Nieman Fellow, 1966; Scripps-Howard Foundation's Distinguished Journalism Citation, 1978; Gerald M. Sass Award for Distinguished Contributions to Journalism Education, 2000; two newspapers under his leadership won Pulitzer Prizes:* Akron Beacon Journal, *1971, and* Detroit News, *1994; honorary doctorate in journalism, DePauw University, 1996; publisher,* Neiman Reports; *author,* Newsroom Management: A Guide to Theory and Practice *(1987).*

Editors' introduction: With American and British troops fighting in Iraq, advocates debated what limits, if any, should be placed upon citizens' rights and practices of free speech. Less than one month after President Bush announced the opening of hostilities against President Saddam Hussein's regime in Iraq, Mr. Giles addressed members of the Cleveland City Club on the importance of free expression. Mr. Giles contended, "The true test of a great democracy is its willingness to protect openness and guarantee the civil liberties of its citizens in the face of threats from abroad." The City Club, a nonpartisan organization, advocates the free expression of all ideas and the benefits of an open exchange. Begun in 1912, the club's programs can be heard across America on hundreds of radio outlets.

Bob Giles' speech: I am delighted to have this opportunity to come home for what is to me the very special honor of addressing this forum.

---

4. Delivered on April 4, 2003, at Cleveland, OH. Reprinted with permission of Bob Giles.

I grew up in a middle class family on the city's far west side near Lakewood. My mom and dad were both college educated, and the living room radio was tuned religiously each week to the broadcasts of the City Club debates.

I wasn't much interested in those broadcasts myself and, looking back, it is inconceivable that my parents could possibly have imagined that their little boy would some day be invited to speak from this podium. Were they still here, they would share my wonder at this occasion.

I have been following the discussion in this community about Supreme Court Justice Antonin Scalia and his demand to the City Club that it exclude radio and television coverage of his speech as a condition of his appearance where he was to be awarded the Citadel of Free Speech Award.

The contradiction with the justice's writings in the Court protecting First Amendment rights is both stark and troubling, as is the decision of this honorable forum of free speech in agreeing to Scalia's demand. With all appropriate respect to my hosts, I want to

---

The true test of a great democracy is its willingness to protect openness and guarantee the civil liberties of its citizens in the face of threats from abroad.

---

add my voice to those who are concerned and disappointed by the justice's instinct to dictate coverage and by the willingness of the City Club to go along.

This troubling episode begs to be seen in a larger framework in which the essential role of the press and the historic values of free expression are being constrained by a government that seeks to manage information and the control of access.

Our democratic system was established on a core belief that a well-informed citizenry was essential to effective functioning of an elected government. This is particularly true in wartime when the country is sending its children into combat, and the citizens at home are seeing for the first time on their television screens live combat scenes that offer a snapshot of the fighting but that also beg for understanding.

We depend on the press to shape a coherent story out of these images through informative dispatches and authoritative analysis. It is the press in its adversarial role that must ask the hard questions that, over time, lead to understanding.

The true test of a great democracy is its willingness to protect openness and guarantee the civil liberties of its citizens in the face of threats from abroad.

A tricky balancing act exists between adherence to the laws and customs of a civil society requiring openness and full representation for the accused, and what the administration is calling the "new reality" that dictates setting aside many of these important democratic conventions as a means of increasing homeland security and preventing future terrorist attacks.

Many Americans see these restrictions as patriotic and target the press itself as a subject of debate and controversy. When their instinct is to rally around their government in times of danger and uncertainty, they expect the press to do the same.

This misunderstands the fundamental role of the press, whose patriotic mission, rather, is to serve as a watchdog for the public on the individuals who hold positions of power in government.

When reporters ask hard questions of a popular administration, forcing Donald Rumsfeld, for example, to defend his wartime strategy, the press is seen by many as being excessively critical, and thus lacking in patriotism when national unity is preferred.

It is understandable that U.S. journalists are deeply patriotic themselves. They tend to be sympathetic toward the soldiers they are writing about and sensitive to the idea many Americans hold that the news media is anti-American.

As people of goodwill discuss the morality and purpose of war, it is important to recognize that we are witnessing a significant transformation in the flow of information that shapes our thinking and our understanding of war.

We could see that this transformation in the nature of journalism was taking place in the weeks leading up to the war; but its pace has been hastened by the onset of the fighting itself.

The technology that is driving this transformation is not new. E-mail and the Internet are familiar tools for moving information and ideas. They are influencing a change in the nature of journalism by bringing into the discussion voices not previously heard, voices not typically noticed by the mainstream news media.

In the weeks leading up to the invasion of Iraq, many of the traditional American forums for discussion and disagreement fell silent. Among them was the absence of robust debate in the legislative branch of the American government.

Members of both political parties, save one, were dissuaded from questioning or challenging the emerging diplomatic and military strategies. They feared disapproval by a popular administration and were said to be intimidated by the prospect of losing favor with voters.

The exception was Senator Robert Byrd, the aging contrarian from West Virginia, who stood in the Senate chamber to chastise his fellows senators for being "ominously, dreadfully silent. There is no debate, no discussion, no attempt to lay out for the nation the pros and cons of this particular war. There is nothing. Only on the editorial pages of our newspapers is there much substantive discussion of the prudence or imprudence of engaging in this particular war."

As hauntingly silent as the Senate might have been, the Internet and e-mail gave life to other voices of dissent and support. Web sites of opinion were bookmarked. List-serves blossomed and became sources for commentary and insight. Every opinion had a chance to be considered.

Dissent expressed through electronic means was vigorous, passionate, and safe. Dissent on the streets of our towns and cities brought the police.

The mainstream news organizations took notice and adjusted their coverage. Both the *New York Times* and the *Washington Post* acknowledged underplaying major antiwar demonstrations and attempted to recover by devoting more coverage to the marching, chanting thousands in the streets.

E-mail and Internet called our attention to other stories missing from daily coverage, including the report in a London paper revealing an internal administration memo calling for the bugging of the offices and homes of the members of the U.S. Security Council.

Another important dimension to this transformation is that television news is taking place on a global platform.

From the beginnings of satellite transmission, television has conveyed a powerful cultural statement about the United States, enabling audiences in other countries to understand us through movies, music, and television entertainment. It wasn't always a pretty picture, but it was essentially a peaceful one.

Satellite transmission invites international viewers to see American journalism in action.

Some of what they see concerns them and raises doubts about the credibility of U.S. television news organizations. The display of the American flag on news broadcasts suggests that the newscasters are simply speaking for the U.S. government, rather than working as journalists with independence and detachment.

International audiences note that the content of news broadcasts focuses heavily on American self-interest. An analysis of 414 stories on the Iraqi question that were aired on NBC, ABC, and CBS from September to February found that the vast majority originated from the White House, Pentagon, and State Department.

Such images convince many that the U.S. press is conformist, rather than free.

Competition and diversity of viewpoints now enlivens a global medium once dominated by American networks, a development that has ramifications for perceptions of the United States and the professionalism of its news media.

The British Broadcasting Corporation has built on a reputation for honesty and accuracy gained during its news broadcasts during World War II when, for listeners in the occupied countries, its radio services were a lifeline.

The BBC continues to fulfill a commitment to international reportage that is grounded in standards for independent neutrality in many ways, including the fact that it offers news in 43 languages.

The growing popularity of BBC among U.S. viewers reflects its growing reputation as a credible and informed option to American newscasts. An impression gained from watching BBC and CNN International during the early days of the war, as I did, is that BBC journalists are more seasoned and knowledgeable.

The Arab world also is tuning into the U.S. news media.

The newspaper *Al Sharq Al Awsat*, which is edited in London and circulated in all Arab countries, carries daily reports, news analysis, and opinion columns from the *New York Times*, the *Washington Post*, the *Los Angeles Times*, and the *Christian Science Monitor*.

Radio Sawa is a U.S.–sponsored 24-hour-a-day Arabic language station that claims to be the number one youth radio station in many Middle Eastern cities. It has just launched an interactive Internet site, www.radiosawa.com.

The most important newcomer on the global news media scene is the all-news Arabic-language news channel Al Jazeera.

It was established in 1996 and receives $30 million in annual support from the government of Qatar but did not command worldwide attention until it broadcast videotaped statements by Osama bin Laden.

Al Jazeera provides a window throughout the Arab world for news from the Middle East, Europe, and America, which is gathered by a large staff of reporters from 30 Arab countries.

BBC recently forged a news-sharing alliance with Al Jazeera, thus enhancing the Arab channel's stature as a legitimate provider of news. And after months of criticism, the Pentagon changed its approach and invited Al Jazeera reporters to join other journalists embedded in U.S. military units in Iraq.

During a seminar for international journalists on media responsibility last month in Salzburg, Austria, the number three editor at Al Jazeera, an Egyptian journalist named Yasser Thabet, showed us videotapes of aggressive, independent coverage that is opening the Arab world to news reports and discussions of topics such as polygamy and democratic reform that are infuriating Arab governments in the region.

The broad complaint against Al Jazeera is that many of its stories and discussions seem to reflect points of view that are hostile to the West. But as many of the international journalists at the seminar asked, can't it be said that American television reflects an American point of view?

Moreover, as Yasser pointed out, the station also interviews Israeli officials and invites American officials to tell their side of the story.

Al Jazeera is being criticized for showing images of captured and dead American and British soldiers. The broadcast of these images set off a round of punitive responses, including a decision to cancel Al Jazeera's credentials at the New York Stock Exchange.

Al Jazeera also has shown images of Iraqi victims and, to Yasser Thabet, such reporting is part of Al Jazeera's efforts to portray the tragic, painful, even bloody side of war.

As Ted Koppel of ABC's *Nightline* observes, "We have an obligation to remind people in the most graphic way that war is a dreadful thing."

Al Jazeera's reach into 35 million homes in the Arab world and its plans to introduce an English-language broadcast foretell a continuing discussion over the differences between its journalistic values and those of U.S. news organizations.

In the current *New Yorker*, an item about a gathering of Arab men who are watching an Al Jazeera broadcast in a café in Brooklyn said the men in the room believed that Al Jazeera provided more reliable information than CNN. This was war, one of them said, with people dying terrible deaths on both sides, but Americans are getting a sanitized picture.

As the *New York Times* observed in an editorial recently, "if our hope for the Arab world is, as the Bush administration never ceases to remind us, for it to enjoy a free, democratic life, Al Jazeera is the kind of television station we should encourage."

The watching world now has a wide choice of news outlets, inviting international audiences to observe U.S. journalism and make its own judgments about the professionalism of news coverage, and how independent and neutral American correspondents and their news organizations appear to be.

The battlefield coverage we are now seeing on our television screens has been shaped by modern information technology. After the Gulf War, journalists complained bitterly that the ability of the press to serve as witness for the public was lost by the confining nature of the reporting pools organized and managed by the Pentagon.

As the war in Iraq approached, the military planners recognized that video and satellite phones would enable journalists to file stories whenever and wherever they wished, in effect talking over the heads of their minders and offering eyewitness evidence of how the war in their sector was going. This realization convinced the Pentagon to provide unprecedented access to combat. The embedded journalists, as we have come to call them, are sending vivid images and written dispatches for readers and viewers around the world.

Giving the press front row seats in Iraq provides an essential counterpoint to the television footage of briefings by Saddam Hussein's ministers as they state their side of the story and show video footage of injured civilians and bombed out buildings that is designed to show U.S. troops as merciless invaders.

As vivid and close-up as the reporting has been, it still is difficult for television to provide a coherent picture of what are essentially chaotic events. Televised coverage of a firefight during the early days of the war was made to seem large when, in fact, it was an episodic event, a small slice of what was going on at that moment, and part of what is being called the fog of war.

In spite of the great strengths of the electronic media, newspapers are doing a better job of helping us digest what has happened. Newspapers are opening up pages for war news every day, providing space for dispatches that provide detail and context, large-scale maps on which we can track the movements of coalition forces and gripping still photography that portrays the brutality of war and the suffering of humanity caught in war.

The *New York Times* noted that this new standard of openness and immediacy raised the question of whether reporters, soldiers, or news consumers will ever be satisfied with less. "The reporters say that they can be objective in their coverage, but that their ability to remain detached is being tested every day by this new level of engagement," the newspaper said.

There is a price to pay for covering combat, of course. While the number of correspondents who are killed, wounded, or captured is mercifully small, this war is likely to produce psychological wounds among the press that cannot go unattended.

Journalists who return to their newsrooms from combat zones or from a posting at the center of terrorist activity find there is little in the way of treatment programs for post-traumatic stress disorder and the possible psychological implications for journalists who spend prolonged periods in zones of conflict.

Until very recently, there was no serious research into the subject. The first such study looking at psychological health of war journalists was completed by Dr. Anthony Feinstein, an associate professor of psychiatry at the University of Toronto.

His findings were published as an article in the September 2002 issue of the *American Journal of Psychiatry* entitled, "A Hazardous Profession: War, Journalists, and Psychopathology."

Dr. Feinstein's study draws its results from 140 war correspondents, men and women, from six major news organizations who regularly covered wars and other armed conflicts.

A significant number of these journalists were severely traumatized, not only by what they experienced but also by what they saw. Their daily lives were disrupted by the post-traumatic stress that remained long after they returned from the battlefields.

The reporters in the study spoke of social difficulties—such things as difficulty adjusting to civil society, a reluctance to engage with friends, damaged relationships, and heightened reliance on alcohol.

He found that the stress levels among war reporters were significantly higher than among those who had not been exposed to combat; nor was there strong evidence to believe that the psychopathology in the study group predated their exposure to war.

Editors had little understanding of the inner perils their correspondents were experiencing, Dr. Feinstein concluded, and few of the journalists independently sought professional help to address the trauma.

Dr. Feinstein's conclusion that war correspondents are at dramatically increased risk of developing severe psychological problems is an important finding, one that merits wide discussion, further examination, and thoughtful attention from editors and news organizations whose correspondents may be in the field for longer periods than was originally thought.

For the first time in the post–Cold War era, perhaps, Americans are getting a clear picture of how their government's foreign and military policies are seen in the rest of the world.

Had U.S. news organizations not shut down foreign news bureaus and brought home correspondents from many areas of the world during the years following the end of the Cold War, Americans would have had a deeper understanding long before September 11 of the building animosity in the Arab world to the policies of our government.

These perceptions are terribly important in a world shrunken by a technology that is no longer just an American phenomenon. These perceptions are shaped by how the world sees America. The battle for the hearts and minds of the Iraqi people, as the administration likes to say, can't be won by armies alone. Our news values are on trial as well before a skeptical and opinionated world jury. Our hearts and minds also may be up for grabs.

Thank you again for giving me this forum to share some thoughts about journalism. I look forward to your questions.

Lou Frey Symposium[5]

Lawrence G. Walters

Partner, Weston, Garrou & DeWitt, www.FirstAmendment.com,
2001– ; born Chicago, IL, November 6, 1963; B.A., University of
Central Florida, 1985; J.D. with honors, College of Law, Florida
State University, 1988; began practicing law in central Florida,
1988; professor of legal studies, University of Central Florida,
1989–94; legal panel, Central Florida ACLU; executive council,
Florida Bar's Public Interest Law Section; founder and chairman,
Florida Bar's First Amendment Law Committee, 1997; director,
Volusia County Bar Association and Deltona Area Chamber of
Commerce, 1992; First Amendment Lawyers Association; created
the Internet Freedom Association, Inc., www.i-freedom.org, a trade
group representing the interests of Web masters across the country;
appeared on 48 Hours, 20/20, Fox Files, O'Reilly Factor, and
Oprah; publishes essays on numerous Web sites and in magazines
and books.

Editors' introduction: Mr. Walters addressed students, teachers, administrators, community leaders, and a few legislators attending the Lou Frey Symposium on Free Speech & Terrorism at the University of Central Florida on "civil liberties after 9/11." Concerned with the government's increased "spying on our own citizens," Mr. Walters warned, "It is important to be on guard against the dilution of civil rights in times of conflict." He also pointed out the irony in trying to bring civil liberties to Iraq while "many are quite willing to deny those same rights to our own citizens when they question our government." Lou Frey, a U.S. congressman from central Florida from 1969 to 1979, founded the Lou Frey Institute of Politics and Government at the University of Central Florida, the unit that sponsored this symposium.

Lawrence G. Walters's speech: Thank you. It's a pleasure to be part of this unique symposium. I am probably not the first speaker to observe that this type of intelligent debate of security issues could not even take place in most countries, so we should feel fortunate to live in a country that historically places such emphasis on civil rights and liberties. Although civil liberties is the last topic on the agenda for this symposium, it should be first and foremost in the minds of lawmakers and justice officials when responding to

---

5. Delivered on April 8, 2003, at Orlando, FL. Reprinted with permission of Lawrence G. Walters.

any type of terrorist threat. Our panel hopes to put the issue of civil liberties in proper perspective in relation to security concerns.

As I said, I practice primarily in the area of constitutional law. I run a Web site called FirstAmendment.com, and my specific mission is to speak to you about civil liberties after 9/11, from the perspective of a practicing attorney.

Before I do that, however, I wanted to note a few interesting facts, which help put some of this in perspective.

1) During the 1980s, polls were taken, and they showed that most American citizens were willing to surrender some Fourth Amendment rights against unreasonable search and seizure, if it would help the drug war. They did surrender those rights, and the Fourth Amendment is a mere shadow of what it once was. Search and seizure law is now a concept riddled with exceptions, almost to the point of becoming meaningless. Law enforcement can now stop and search you just about any time, so long as they're willing to recite the right boilerplate in their arrest affidavits. The Fourth Amendment all but died, but drugs are still going strong. There has not been a significant reduction in either the supply or the demand for drugs. Yet the damage to Fourth Amendment rights is irreversible.

Fast forward to present day . . .

2) According to a recent *Time* magazine poll, 47 percent of American citizens think that the government should violate their rights if it would help the war on terrorism.

Some of them will not have to wait very long, with the enactment of the PATRIOT Act, soon possibly PATRIOT Act II, data mining, secret foreign intelligence courts, and sneak and peak search warrants. For the first time in decades, the Justice Department has repealed the Levy guidelines, and reinstated spying on our own citizens, without probable cause. Suspected terrorists are stripped of all semblance of due process and held without charges or access to counsel, like Jose Padilla, who has yet to be charged or convicted of a crime. Once private e-mail communications may now be intercepted by the government with reduced judicial oversight, even though the courts approve virtually all requests for wiretaps and warrants sought by the government, sometimes with the weakest of evidence.

I heard Ric Keller say yesterday that this is just not happening, so take comfort. Well the problem with that is we don't know if it's happening or not. The PATRIOT Act and the FISA allow these types of searches of our e-mail and on-line activities, but the warrants and legal proceedings are not made public. The Freedom of Information Act does not apply to these proceedings, so the public is never informed of any potential abuses of the system. The issue is not whether the abuses are occurring, from a constitutional perspective, the issue is whether they *can* occur! To mix a metaphor, our freedom should not depend on the kindness of strangers!

3) The next point is more of an observation than a fact. But it appears to me in both my dealings with the public, the media, and the courts, that any form of dissent or protest against the current U.S. international policy is seen as "unpatriotic" instead of a minority viewpoint. Several conservative commentators have even suggested trying war protesters and some journalists for treason, as a result of expressing opposition to the current conflict in Iraq. Whitehouse Spokesman Ari Fleischer gave a chilling warning shortly after 9/11, that Americans ought to "watch what they say, and watch what they do."

Some media outlets will grudgingly admit that the protesters and the press have First Amendment protection, to some minimal degree; many others have taken an extremely hostile approach to those who do not agree with current governmental policy. Let me give you an example: I appeared last week as a guest on the *O'Reilly Factor*, where I was joined by another guest, Paul Kent, who is a spokesman for the Southeastern Legal Foundation. Mr. Kent seriously supported trying Peter Arnett for treason, for providing an interview to the Iraqi media. While this interview may have been a mistake on various levels, it hardly rises to the level of criminal treason. It is this kind of knee-jerk reaction against which we must be most on guard.

Ironically, our goal in Iraq is to bring some semblance of civil liberties to this oppressed nation, but many are quite willing to deny those same rights to our own citizens when they question our government. The ability to openly criticize our leaders is a uniquely democratic right, and a liberty that is cherished in any free society. Often in wartime, this civil right is endangered, as it is now.

> *What we're seeing is an* **unfortunate** *disregard for basic civil rights by both prosecutors and the judiciary.*

All this sets the stage for what's occurring in the courts . . .

So how are First Amendment rights seen by the judges and juries? Of course I can only provide you a snapshot view from my practice, but I can tell you that many other civil rights lawyers report experiences similar to mine:

What we're seeing is an *unfortunate* disregard for basic civil rights by both prosecutors and the judiciary. While there are certainly exceptions to this rule, I have been troubled by how First Amendment rights are often being given nothing more than lip service in the courts. Concepts like law and order, security, and morality get significant attention in the court system, while constitutional rights are often seen as a nuisance to be overcome, or avoided. Even 5 years ago, when we would go into court with the First Amendment on our side, we would meet with a very favorable reception by judges and juries. Disturbingly, I now see allegations that we're trying to "wrap ourselves in the First Amendment" or "hide behind the Bill of Rights." Of course civil rights are supposed to provide "protection" and "cover" from governmental overreaching, but there is definitely an increased hostility toward any sort of constitutional law arguments since 9/11.

Of course, federal courts are often more sensitive to constitutional law arguments than state courts, but that's not always true either. With so many conservative federal judges having been appointed by recent Republican presidents, the previous sensitivity to civil rights is also going by the wayside.

It is important to be on guard against the dilution of civil rights in times of conflict. While it is certainly appropriate to support our troops fighting on foreign soil to make the world a safer place, we must never forget that many died before them to preserve our Constitution and liberties. Freedom is never free, but comes as the price of eternal vigilance. Fortunately, our liberties have withstood greater tests of time than the current conflicts in the Middle East. The Bill of Rights survived the Civil War, and two World Wars. The War on Terrorism is not as great a threat to our country as either of those conflicts. While many commentators and politicians are keen

> *The right to dissent, to speak freely, to live in private, and petition the government become even more important in times of military conflict.*

to say that "everything changed after 9/11," that is only partly true. We certainly feel more vulnerable to foreign extremist groups, but this tragedy must not be used as a pretext for stripping away civil liberties.

Unfortunately, there are those in power who have sought to do just that. While the government has the obligation to protect its citizens from legitimate threats, the existence of some threat does not provide a valid basis to put civil liberties on the back burner. The right to dissent, to speak freely, to live in private, and petition the government become even more important in times of military conflict. The stakes are higher, and people feel stronger about their positions.

I want to save some time for questions and other panelists, but the last concept I would note is the one-sidedness of the television talk show format. I need not tell you that television influences many minds in current society. Most people get their news from television, as opposed to newspapers, magazines, or other media. For years, conservatives have complained about the "liberal media." However, the pendulum has certainly swung the other direction now, and it is currently difficult if not impossible to find a liberal talk show host. This imbalance has contributed to the era of hostility when it comes to civil rights. War protesters and other dissenters have been demonized by the conservative talk show hosts, to the point where there is a legitimate fear of questioning the government out on the streets.

The good news is that the opposing voice has adopted the Internet as its medium of choice for communications. The world was amazed when individuals from many countries were able to organize antiwar protests involving millions of people taking to the streets worldwide, on the same day! The courts have called the Internet the "most participatory form of mass communication yet developed." Judges have consistently struck down attempts to censor or regulate the content of communications on-line. The Web has been seen as somewhat of a "sacred cow," which the courts are hesitant to slaughter. It may be that the dissenting, critical voice will have to be happy with the Internet as its forum of choice for now. Of course, inroads should be made into the mainstream media to ensure a balanced presentation. But for now, the Internet has proved to be a last bastion of freedom, to a certain extent. Robust debate on all these issues takes place every day in chat rooms, news groups, and by e-mail. It may be that traditional media will become less and less important as time goes on and the computer terminal becomes the primary source for information, replacing the television screen.

The other piece of good news, from a civil liberties standpoint, is that membership in the ACLU has reached record levels, with even some former staunch conservatives becoming concerned enough about the erosion of civil liberties to join the ACLU. Typically, when civil rights have been in trouble in the past, the American people have risen to the occasion and demanded adherence to the Constitution by the courts, the military, and law enforcement. We're now seeing signs that people have had enough, and have started to demand protection for our cherished civil liberties. The fact of this seminar occurring is an extremely positive development. Only through intelligent debate can civil liberties endure in an environment where we can remain safe as well.

In closing, I would only remind you of the apt quote from Benjamin Franklin: "Those who would give up essential liberty to purchase a little temporary safety deserve neither liberty nor safety."

Thank you.

Combating Terrorism, Preserving Freedom[6]

Timothy Lynch

Director, The Cato Institute's Project on Criminal Justice; B.A. in economics, Marquette University; J.D., Marquette University School of Law, 1990; specializes in issues relating to the criminal justice system, the Constitution, and the Bill of Rights; joined Cato Institute, 1991; authored articles in New York Times, Wall Street Journal, Washington Post, National Law Journal, *and elsewhere; appeared on* The NewsHour with Jim Lehrer, NBC Nightly News, ABC World News Tonight, The O'Reilly Factor, *and* C-SPAN's Washington Journal.

Editors' introduction: After the terrorist attacks of 9/11, while leaders explored ways of preventing similar tragedies in the future, others considered what limits, if any, should be placed upon the debate concerning how best to defeat terrorism. Mr. Lynch explores the question, "How do we respond to the threat of terrorism without surrendering . . . freedoms?" He concludes, "Our government should be focusing its attention on how to alter Al Qaeda's way of life, not our own." Founded in 1977, the Cato Institute is a nonprofit public policy research foundation, headquartered in Washington, D.C., that seeks to broaden the parameters of public policy debate to allow consideration of the traditional American principles of limited government, individual liberty, free markets, and peace.

Timothy Lynch's speech: The September 11th attacks demonstrated to the world that members of the Al Qaeda terrorist network are willing to sacrifice themselves to slaughter thousands of innocent people. The problem that we have on our hands could not be more serious. We all want the government to do its very best to catch these terrorists before they commit any more atrocities. The challenge is this: How do we respond to the threat of terrorism without surrendering the freedoms that have made America the greatest country in all of world history?

My observations, analysis, and conclusions are going to be nonpartisan and long-term in nature. To me, this is not about President Bush, and it is not about Attorney General John Ashcroft. And it is not about which political party controls the Congress. The legal pre-

---

6. Delivered on April 14, 2003, at The Cato Institute Hill Briefing and broadcast live on C-SPAN, Capitol Hill, Washington, D.C. Reprinted with permission of Timothy Lynch.

cedents that are being set now transcend the present players. The real issue is the power of government, and what are going to be the limits on that power.

I think President Bush did the right thing when he dispatched our military forces to Afghanistan. It was a wise move because it was going right at the root of the problem, which is Osama bin Laden, the Taliban, and the terrorist base camps. However, I think President Bush has been getting a lot of bad advice on how to handle the terrorist problem here at home. As most of you know, the debate here at home has been framed in terms of "liberty and security." The basic argument seems to be that civilians have been slaughtered and the slaughter is proof that the government doesn't have enough power to stop such atrocities from happening. So policymakers must redraw the line between "liberty and security" to make sure that such atrocities don't happen again. The argument has been made, What good is liberty when Al Qaeda is coming at us with weapons of mass destruction? I think framing the debate in that way is a serious mistake. And I want to suggest an alternative framework for your consideration. There is not enough time for me to present a compelling case, but what I hope to do is give you some things to think about when this session is over.

There are plenty of things the government can do to make us safer without impinging upon civil liberties.

My framework for responding to the problem of terrorism consists of four principles. First, restricting our freedom is not the only option open to policymakers. Second, before we confer more power on the government, let's assess how well it is using the powers it already has. Third, if more power must be given, let us proceed cautiously and prudently. Fourth, at some point, all friends of liberty have to recognize that if we're serious about keeping our freedom, there has to be some point where we say "enough." At some point, we must stop redrawing this line between "liberty and security" because if we do not take a stand, eventually we're not going to have any freedom left.

Now let me elaborate a bit more on these points. Going back to the first principle, which is: Restricting our freedom is not the only policy option available. This point has to be stressed because when the debate or discussion is framed in terms of "liberty and security," the implication is that if we want to take any action to make ourselves more secure, we have to focus on restricting one of our civil liberties. That is very misleading. There are plenty of things the government can do to make us safer without impinging upon civil liberties. Let me give you a few examples. The government can shore up our woefully inadequate civil defense system. We at the Cato Institute have been very critical of the policy of stockpiling the smallpox vaccine, for example. We think the vaccine should be made widely available to the public because that would accomplish two important objectives. First, it can deter a terrorist attack. Al Qaeda is seeking to inflict massive casualties. But the smallpox virus cannot spread in a widely vaccinated population. So we should get that vaccine out and available to the public right now. That would remove a very tempting target for the terrorists. Second, by making the vaccine available, that would allow each of us, individually, to take some actions to protect ourselves and our family members without leaving us dependent upon the Department of Health and Human Services, which is certainly the case if the government continues its policy of stockpiling the vaccine. Stockpiling puts America in a reactive posture and makes us dependent on the government to make ourselves safe.

In the realm of foreign policy, we also think it is a very big mistake for our government to be so cozy with Saudi Arabia. Our national security adviser, Condoleezza Rice, likes to say that our foreign policy should reflect our values. And she's right, it should. But in Saudi Arabia, criticism of the government is completely banned. Conversion to Christianity is not only a crime, it's punishable by the death penalty. We heard a lot about the plight of women in Afghanistan before our troops went there. But the situation of women in Saudi Arabia isn't a lot better. Women, for example, cannot leave the country without the permission of their father, their husband, or a brother. The Saudi government was also not helpful to our government when our troops there were attacked in a terrorist incident a few years ago. The Saudi government did not help our government identify who was responsible and help us to track them down. It has also come to light that there's been money from the royal family that has actually been going into terrorist networks. And our troop presence there does more harm than good, because it unnecessarily inflames terrorists who then want to seek vengeance on Americans here at home. Recall that fourteen or fifteen of the nineteen hijackers on September 11 were young Saudi men.

On the local level, policymakers can do a better job of improving the coordination of the police departments and the fire departments. Jim Dwyer, a reporter with the *New York Times*, has been doing a terrific job writing about this problem—especially with respect to what happened on September 11th and in its aftermath. Dwyer points out that when the fire department went to the Twin Towers, it set up the command post at the base of the towers. New York City police officers were in helicopters way up above where the planes hit the towers and they could clearly see the raging fire, and they could tell that it was just a matter of time before those towers collapsed. The problem was that the police could not get that information to the firefighters, who were inside resting in the stairwells. Now, my point here is not to say that this was poor performance. My point is that this problem of lack of coordination has not been fixed. Mayor Bloomberg inexplicably decided to have the departments evaluated separately after September 11th. The mayor had one team evaluate the police department and he had another team evaluate the fire department. The mayor should have taken a holistic approach. The main point here is that this unfixed problem of coordination between the police and the fire department could end up costing many lives in some future emergency.

Let me now turn to the second principle, which is: Before we confer more power to the government, let's assess how well the government has been using its existing powers. I have to say that there are serious problems at the FBI. There are misplaced priorities, there's dereliction of duty, there's incompetence, and in some cases there's actual illegal conduct. We all saw the newspapers last week where we discovered that FBI counterespionage officials have been sleeping with a Chinese double agent. According to the reports, those agents left classified information unprotected. Even worse, their supervisors seem to have missed or ignored red flags that were raised about that woman years ago. I'm sure we'll be hearing more about that in the weeks and months to come.

Let me give you another example. There was an FBI agent in the Arizona office—this is the one who sent the memo to FBI headquarters that said, "We ought to canvass all of the American flight schools. I think there's a problem. I think there's a terrorist plot under way." How many people here know that this one agent was one of five in that office who were assigned to international terrorism problems? And yet there are fifty agents in that office who spend their days and weeks trying to track down marijuana smugglers. That is what I mean by the FBI's misplaced priorities.

Third, I don't know how many people here saw the eye-opening episode of *60 Minutes* last October on the problem in the translation department over at the FBI. This is an episode that you just had to see for yourself in order to believe it.

You know that after the September 11 attacks the FBI director appealed to the public and said, "we need help with translators—people who understand the Arabic language, please apply to the FBI, there's a shortage here." So the Bureau did hire a lot of people. Remember that in the weeks immediately after 9/11 you have FBI agents out in the field who are working overtime trying to track down leads, trying to find out if there are more terrorist sleeper cells right here in America planning additional attacks. Those FBI agents are sending information on a daily basis back to headquarters saying, "Can you please translate this wiretap?" Or, "we found these documents in a search of this apartment. Will you please translate this, let us know what it means, and get back to us as soon as possible?" Meanwhile, back at FBI headquarters, there was a translator who was hired shortly after 9/11. She wanted to work overtime too, in order to respond to these requests that were coming in by the FBI field agents. As unbelievable as it may sound, her supervisor encouraged her not only not to work overtime, but also to take longer lunch breaks, to take longer coffee breaks. This supervisor went so far as to destroy work that the translator had been doing. The translator would come into the office the next day and discover that all the translating work that she had done the previous day had been deleted from her computer. And the explanation that she told to *60 Minutes* was that her supervisor said, "How are we ever going to get a bigger budget from the Congress if we're getting all of this work done? If we can show Congress piles of unfinished work, we will be able to get a bigger budget and we'll get more staff members for our division."

Now this woman just couldn't believe this, so she became a whistleblower, and tried to bring the problem to the attention of FBI managers, to members of Congress, and finally to the news media and *60 Minutes*. Now, you would think that this translator would have been given a medal and her supervisor would have been fired. Just the opposite happened. This woman, who was trying to raise the alarm about this problem, she was fired from the FBI! We have to keep these problems in mind when we're talking about conferring more power to the federal government. If this type of nonsense is happening behind the walls of FBI headquarters, what good is giving more power to this agency going to do? Is it really going to give us more safety?

One final point about the FBI. There has been illegal conduct at the FISA court. "FISA" stands for Foreign Intelligence Surveillance Act, and the FBI agents go to the FISA court in order to get special wiretaps and special search warrants in terrorism-related investigations. One FBI agent filed so many false and misleading affidavits to the FISA court that the court took the extraordinary step of barring this agent from ever appearing before the court again. Now, I don't know how many people here are lawyers, but the lawyers will know that this is an extraordinary step by a court, which means this agent stepped far over the line by filing these false and misleading affidavits. Now, you would think that the agent would be indicted for perjury—and yet, there has been no accountability whatsoever for that agent.

These problems raise the question as to whether the federal police agencies are properly exercising the powers that they already have. If they are not, does it make sense to reward them with bigger budgets and even more power?

Turning now to principle number three, which is: If more power must be conferred to the government, let us move cautiously and prudently, not hastily. There are good ways to make laws and there are bad ways to make laws. And the PATRIOT Act is a textbook example on how not to make law. Attorney General John Ashcroft came to the Congress and said, "I want this antiterrorism bill enacted"—and his proposal was one of these telephone directory book–sized bills that are cobbled together—and Ashcroft said, "I want this passed in three days." Even supporters of the administration said, "That's just not going to happen." So then Ashcroft said, "Ok, let's pass it in two weeks." Many people responded by saying, "Look, this is a large, complicated piece of legislation. Parts of it aren't controversial at all. Let's break it down into some smaller parts. We can immediately enact the parts everybody agrees on. Why not enact those into law right away, and slow this down, and take a closer look at some of the more controversial provisions." The administration wouldn't have any of it. Bush and his people wanted to keep all of the proposals in one package, and voted up or down. Supporters of the measure decided to call it the

> *Let's not make the same mistakes we made with the first PATRIOT Act.*

"PATRIOT Act" to intimidate any of the people who were raising any questions or concerns about it.

Then some skeptics said, "If this legislation is so urgent that it must be enacted immediately, let's attach sunset provisions to the law. That way we'll confer the powers that the attorney general says law enforcement agents need, but we'll have the law expire after, say, two years, so that we can assess exactly how the new law is being used, whether it's really necessary, and if it's not, the law will expire. But if it is really necessary, then, presumably, it will garner enough support in the Congress so it will pass again." Again, sunset proposals were resisted very fiercely by the administration. We ended up having some sunset provisions on some parts of the PATRIOT Act, but the important point is that these were over the objections of the administration. Some of their supporters on Capitol Hill said, "Look, you cannot object to this. It's a very reasonable thing. You cannot object to it." So, a few sunset provisions were enacted, but it was over the objections of the administration. But even now the administration is working quietly with a few members of Congress to have those sunset provisions removed and to make the PATRIOT Act permanent.

I fully agree with the defense and intelligence experts who say that it is only a matter of time before America is attacked again. When America is attacked again, it's very likely that we will see another big, antiterrorism proposal submitted to the Congress. We're already seeing reports of "PATRIOT II" that have been leaked out of the government. The important points here are, let's not make the same mistakes we made with the first PATRIOT Act. First, these gigantic, telephone directory–sized bills should be considered completely unacceptable. Such proposals should be broken down into smaller parts and voted on separately. The provisions that have merit will garner a majority of Congress and they can be enacted into law. But keeping proposals in gigantic, omnibus packages increases the chances of bad or unwise provisions being enacted into law. Policymakers should also insist on sunset provisions. No reasonable objection can be made, in my view, to breaking these things down into smaller parts and insisting on sunset provisions. If the administration insists on disregarding both of these procedural safeguards, everybody who is concerned about liberty should know that we're about to see a law enacted in the name of political expediency, not real security.

Let me turn, finally, to the fourth principle, which is: if we are serious about keeping our liberty, we have to, at some point, say that the government must do the best it can with the powers that it already has. Because if we don't draw that line in the sand somewhere, if we keep redrawing this line between "liberty and security" every time America is attacked, everybody has to admit that at some point, it may not be five years from now, it might be fifteen, twenty, thirty years from now, we're going to have a lot less liberty than we do today.

I think our elected officials here in Washington do not give the American people enough credit. I think if America is attacked again, and the president, whoever he is, whether it's President George Bush or his successor, if the president were to exhibit leadership and declare, "We're going to track down the people who are responsible for this attack. But we're not going to surrender any more of our freedom." I really think that, by-and-large, the American people would accept that course of action.

Let me summarize my main points. It is a serious mistake to think of our dilemma as one of "liberty versus security." I suggest the following framework of four principles. First, restricting our freedom is not the only policy option. We have to keep this in mind when America is attacked again. Too often we just rush into the legislative process and start asking the wrong questions, such as "What's in the antiterrorism bill, what's it going to do, so-on-and-so-forth." We should make sure that other options have been exhausted before we turn on our civil liberties and reach the conclusion that there's too much freedom and too much privacy in America. Second, before we confer more power, let's assess how well the government has been using its existing powers. This nonsense with the translators at FBI headquarters is totally unacceptable. Congress should not be increasing the budget of the FBI year in and year out when we're hearing such awful stories. Third, if more power must be conferred, let's move cautiously and prudently, not hastily. I hope we've learned a lesson from the first PATRIOT Act experience. Policymakers who care about liberty must insist on breaking gigantic "antiterrorism" bills down into smaller parts so that they can be analyzed closely. And policymakers should also insist on sunset provisions. Fourth, as I just mentioned, there has to come a point when we have to say that we're not going to surrender any more of our liberty. We want the government to fight the terrorists, but they must do the best they can with their existing powers.

On the very day of the September 11th attacks, Secretary of Defense Donald Rumsfeld said, "We have to be careful not to allow the terrorists to alter our way of life." Rumsfeld was exactly right about that. Sometimes the proper response is just to send our military directly to the source. Our government should be focusing its attention on how to alter Al Qaeda's way of life, not our own. Thank you very much.

IV. The Welfare of Children

Children's Behavioral Health Conference on "What Works"[1]

Douglas W. Nelson

President, Annie E. Casey Foundation, 1990– ; grew up in Chicago, IL; bachelor's degree, University of Illinois, 1968; M.A. in history, University of Wyoming; professor, American social history, University of Wisconsin; speech writer, Governor Patrick Lacey of Wisconsin; head, Wisconsin Department on Aging; assistant secretary, Wisconsin Department of Health and Social Services; deputy director, Center for the Study of Social Policy, 1986–90; U.S. delegate to World Conference of Ministers Responsible for Youth, 1998; member, American Bar Association's Commission on the Legal Problems of the Elderly; program adviser, Edna McConnell Clark Foundation; on boards of various social services organizations; lectures, addresses, and writes on wide range of domestic social policy issues; author, Heart Mountain, *nominated for Pulitzer Prize, 1976.*

Editors' introduction: Since 1948, the Annie E. Casey Foundation (AECF) has worked to foster public policies, human service reforms, and community supports that more effectively meet the needs of today's vulnerable children and families. Over the years, President Nelson has spoken on these issues, as he did in this speech to the conference sponsored by the Maine Children's Alliance. President Nelson concluded that the "systems that were created to address the needs of young persons who are emotionally, behaviorally, and psychologically challenged . . . just plain don't work," while other programs "are very often simply not available." President Nelson outlined seven "principles" that "provide a helpful starting point for the complex task of system redesign."

Douglas W. Nelson's speech: Thank you. First of all, I want to congratulate the Maine Children's Alliance on last night's really grand event recognizing some exceptional individuals and organizations—what the alliance calls Champions for Children—several of whom were singled out for their first-rate work with young people with emotional, behavioral, and learning disorders.

Second, I want to express my admiration for the planning behind the two-day event we're kicking off this morning. I'm impressed with the breadth of public-private sponsorship behind this confer-

---

1. Delivered on May 15, 2002, at Portland, ME. Reprinted with permission of Douglas W. Nelson.

ence—providers, state agencies, advocates, parents, insurers, consumers, and the professions. Real change in how we meet the behavioral health needs of children, youth, and families is going to require just this kind of coalition and consensus building across sectors, across categorical funding streams, across the gulf that often divides professionals from consumers, and across disciplines and therapeutic approaches. This breadth is a necessary condition for building the kind of broadly shared vision that is required for meaningful reform of supports to troubled kids and families.

I am also impressed with the degree of experience, innovation, and expertise reflected in the range of workshops being offered over the next two days. I know just enough about some presenters and just enough about some of the imaginative work they do to guarantee you that you will learn a lot more from these sessions—and a lot more than you are going to learn from me in this opening.

That admission might make a wiser man be still. But I never met a podium I could resist and I never passed up the chance to express an opinion or two on what's wrong with the big systems in this country—the systems that were created to address the needs of young persons who are emotionally, behaviorally, and psychologically challenged.

The simple truth is there is a lot wrong. Above all, for lots of people, these systems just plain don't work. They don't prevent problems from going from bad to worse. Once problems are acknowledged, the interventions or treatments or help these systems commonly extend don't yield real relief, rehabilitation, recovery, or even real amelioration. For those who do benefit, too often the benefits are left unsecured by adequate follow-up and reinforcement or continuity and, as a result, they dissipate.

I should add (and perhaps I should emphasize) that the systems of help, whatever their value, are very often simply not available to those who need help the most. They are not available because they are unaffordable or inaccessible or oversubscribed or in English only. They are not available because the kid is not Medicaid eligible or because Dad's insurance does not cover it, or because the Department of Mental Health says it's really a child welfare case, or because the child welfare agency says this is a special education responsibility, or because the innovative community program that could help just lost its grant funding from some foundation with a short attention span.

Maybe this is enough to establish there's something wrong with our big systems for addressing behavioral health issues. Maybe I should layoff. But I can't—not just yet. I can't resist mentioning two additional things. First, these systems cost a lot—they cost billions in hard-to-get public and private dollars—year in and year out. And second, there is almost no fixed accountability for the fact these systems don't return much in the way of real human and health results for the vast investments made in them and through them.

But none of what I said these last few minutes is as noteworthy as what I'm about to contend. And that is this: These terribly broken systems are full of knowledge; they are populated by smart, caring doctors, caseworkers, aides, clinicians, counselors, and teachers. They include creative interventions, effective therapies, sound pharmaceutical treatments, innovative programs and approaches, instructive experiments, good casework, and intelligent preventive strategies.

Put another way, the failure of these systems is not the clinical professional's fault, it's not the insurance company's fault, it's not the Medicaid director's fault, it's not the mental health commissioner's fault, it's not the school board's fault, it's not the residential program's fault, or the fault of the psychiatric hospitals, or the boot camp initiative; it's not the fault of the legislators or lobbyists or advocates who care most about behavioral health. And it's surely not the fault of well-intended foundations that have helped support new services and programs over the years.

> *Child welfare, juvenile justice, mental health, special education . . . are the products of 50 years of disastrously uncoordinated good intentions.*

No, no one of us deserves the blame for the frustratingly inefficient and ineffective and expensive behavioral health systems that exist in most states. It's not the fault of any one of us, *but* it most surely is the fault of *all* of us.

I think this is critically important to acknowledge as a first step toward reform. The search for scapegoats, the search for fall guys, the search for bad motives just won't get us very far.

The real truth is that these systems—which are in need of so much repair—child welfare, juvenile justice, mental health, special education—they are not the creations of bad intentions or indifference. Instead, they are the products of 50 years of disastrously uncoordinated good intentions. These systems today are a crazy quilt of conflicting ideas, theories, philosophies, and treatment modalities. They reflect the partial triumphs of the preventionists and the advocates for deep-end kids. They are the product of those who favor least restricted settings and those who argue for structure and isolation. There are parts of these systems created by the champions of specialization that stand along side parts created by the advocates for integration and mainstreaming. There are behaviorists who share case management responsibilities with psychoanalysts. They are part medical model, part social model, part no model.

These systems were not built by coherent design, but by piecemeal increments. In response to new ideas, fads, newly recognized needs, publicized crises, and frenzies of narrow advocacy, we have layered on new initiatives, new funding streams, new fiscal incentives, new target populations, new eligibility rules, new providers, new practice standards—and we've usually done this without taking any of the earlier pieces away.

The result is not unlike a house built by scores of architects and scores of contractors all building rooms without much regard to what anyone else has constructed. In the end it's not surprising that systems we find ourselves living in today are home to dizzying fragmentation, duplication, huge gaps, conflicting styles, contradictory practices and protocols, and intense competition. And it really should be no surprise that the whole thing, the whole behavioral health system, is seen and experienced as a dizzying and impenetrable maze to the very kids and families it was intended to help.

I've engaged in this diatribe at some length because I think the most useful advice I can give at the outset of this conference is to urge you not to try and fix Maine's behavioral health systems by agreeing to add one or two more new rooms to it. I just don't think it will help, however grand the new rooms might be.

Instead, I urge you to think about fundamentally reconceiving, redesigning, and over time thoroughly and consistently renovating the house you have all inherited—from the ground up.

I know this is a daunting task. For ten years the Casey Foundation has been working with state human service systems, with innovative programs, with thoughtful evaluators, with practitioners, and with families and kids trying to figure out this renovation process and trying to identify the key design principles for systems that would work better.

We don't have a blueprint yet, but we do have some conclusions, some hopefully informed biases, and a sketch at least of the characteristics that might just make for a more effective system. Let me briefly share them.

First of all, we have concluded that real reform requires that all the stakeholders in the existing system find the courage to admit that it is fundamentally broken . . . that it just plain isn't working. This acknowledgment, by the way, has to go beyond saying: What I'm doing is fine, it's what everybody else is doing that is broken. That point of view is a guarantee that the status quo will be maintained.

Secondly, key stakeholders have to agree that to truly fix the system we've got to be willing to think radically, fundamentally, unselfishly about a new way of meeting kid and family needs. More specifically, we've got to be willing to struggle toward a new consensus about how these services are organized and integrated, how they are financed, the way and the places that services are delivered, the way case plans are made and implemented, and what exactly are the key outcomes for kids and families the system ought to be held accountable for achieving. Arriving at such a consensus is absolutely critical and requires real political leadership and stakeholder courage.

Furthermore, while we need to begin this system reform process at the roots, we don't really have to start with a blank slate. We know a lot, we are learning a lot, and the experience of the people in this room doubtlessly includes many of the key principles, values, and goals needed to inform a thoughtful redesign of the system.

From the Casey Foundation's experience, for example, we've come to believe that a few critical principles provide a helpful starting point for the complex task of system redesign. I offer these Casey findings not as a recommendation, but as a provocation to your own thinking.

The number one principle is that we have got to make improved lives, improved health, the success of kids and families the paramount goal or outcome of behavioral health systems. That is, we have to go beyond a focus on isolated symptoms, on diagnosable

---

We have got to make improved lives, improved health, the success of kids and families the paramount goal or outcome of behavioral health systems.

---

disease, on personal deficits, or on the well-being of our agency and program and professions as the ultimate object of the system. The real measure of a behavioral health system's success is whether it helps people at risk lead the lives they aspire to.

The second principle is that kids and adults lead their lives—not in isolation—but in families, in communities, in economies, in cultures, and in social relations. Helping people lead healthier lives means learning to deliver support and treatment in the context of family, community, culture, and key social relations. This tells us a lot about what we do wrong now and where and how and with whom we have to intervene to do better.

Third, healthy lives are not lived in one-hour sessions, or 28-day stays, or even in school years. Healthy development, and the mastering of challenges, is a continuous and organic process. We have simply got to make the processes of intervention and support in the lives of challenged people more continuous, more seamless, more natural—if we expect our support to make more of a difference in people's lives.

The fourth principle is that we have to find a way to coordinate and make mutually reinforcing the diverse range of help and treatment and expertise that some severely challenged kids require. We can't build healthier lives with seven case managers and four reimbursement streams. Hard as it's going to be, we have to put a single face, a single point of accountability on how the system delivers help to multiple problem kids and families.

Fifth, we need to act on the lessons of research and experience, and focus more of behavioral health and family support interventions early in the evolution of life-compromising problems. In other words, we have to make proven prevention and early intervention programs a focus of system investments and not a footnote.

Sixth, new and better systems will have to more fully recognize that kids and families are primary stakeholders in their own lives and health and aspirations. We have to acknowledge that more, respect that more, and recognize the power in it. Put simply, the decision-making in the planning of cases and the delivery of services has to be shared more with the kids and families we are seeking to help.

And finally, any new system we build has to incorporate continuous and honest feedback on effects and on results. We can't continue to tolerate good intentions. We can't continue to let proven interventions coexist with practices and treatments that show no results. In short, we have to insist on a system that rewards and builds on "what works" and abandons those efforts that don't.

These are a few of the architectural principles that shape the Casey Foundation's thinking about the renovation of our behavior health systems. There are doubtlessly others; there may well be more important ones. I offer them this morning not as a prescription, but simply to recommend that any serious reform has to begin with a commitment to building consensus on the purposes, the values, the principles that will make for a truly better continuum of care for kids and families. There is no more important step in the reform process.

In closing this brief sermon, let me make a bit of an apology. I'm fully aware that the critique and advice I've so crudely offered is a little bit draconian, daunting, radical, and difficult. I wish I could be otherwise. By temperament I am an incrementalist and a moderate. I wish there were a short, easy fix that would close the gap between what we want our behavioral health programs to do for kids and what those programs are actually doing.

But I don't believe an easy course is available and I think too much is at stake in the lives of too many kids to avoid taking the longer, harder road to real reform.

My one consolation in making this case is where I'm making it. Maine's got lots of assets. Smart, committed people, quality advocates, innovative programs, good leadership, a track record of achievement on other tough challenges, and a manageable scale of problems and populations—compared to lots of other places.

Somebody has got to show the country the way on this very hard journey, and few are better positioned than you all are to give it a constructive try.

I'd like to think that this conference might just someday be seen as a key step on that critical journey.

I wish you well, and thanks for having me.

Understanding Adoption: A View for Psychiatrists[2]

Adam Pertman

Executive director, Evan B. Donaldson Adoption Institute, 2002– ; born Wroclaw, Poland, February 13, 1953; emigrated with family to United States, December 1958; senior reporter and editor, Boston Globe, *1978–2001; founder, Adoption Nation Education Initiative, 2002; nominated for Pulitzer Prize for a series of articles in* Boston Globe, *"The Adoption Revolution," 1998; Angel in Adoption Award, U.S. Congress, 2002; Special Friend of Children Award, American Academy of Child and Adolescent Psychiatrists, 2002; Friend of Adoption Award, ODS Adoption Community of New England; Century Foundation's Leonard Silk Journalism Award; author* Adoption Nation: How the Adoption Revolution Is Transforming America *(2000), named Book of the Year by the National Adoption Foundation; commentaries in* Los Angeles Times, Boston Globe, Baltimore Sun, Miami Herald; *has appeared on many radio and television programs, including National Public Radio,* Oprah, *and* Today.

Editors' introduction: Founded in 1996, the Evan B. Donaldson Adoption Institute, for which Mr. Pertman is executive director, is a national nonprofit organization whose mission is to improve the quality of information about adoption, enhance the understanding and perception of adoption, and advance adoption policy and practice. In this speech, drawing from experiences adopting his own children and writing extensively about adoption, Mr. Pertman expresses his concern that "we, as a culture and as individuals, . . . have barely begun to recognize or attempt to correct the negative repercussions of adoption's legacy of secrecy, stigmas, and shame." He spoke upon receiving the Special Friend of Children Award from the American Academy of Child and Adolescent Psychiatrists. The event, held at the Massachusetts Medical Society headquarters in Waltham, MA, was the annual banquet of the New England Council of Child and Adolescent Psychiatrists, the organization that nominated him for the award.

Adam Pertman's speech: Good evening. I can't begin to tell you how flattered I am to be here tonight and to receive this award. I'd

---

2. Delivered on June 5, 2002, at Waltham, MA. Reprinted with permission of Adam Pertman.

like to thank Sharon Weinstein, in particular, for being so gracious, so kind, and, of course, so deluded as to think that I deserve it.

Seriously, I'm delighted to be here partly because everyone likes to have his or her work recognized. But that's not the primary reason. Rather, I view this honor as a significant sign of how far adoption has come in its journey out of the dark shadows of American culture, and I see it as a clear indication of your interest in and concern about an issue that I care passionately about. For those two big reasons, you cannot imagine how grateful I am. Thank you all very much.

I thought I'd start off with a psychiatrist joke; God bless the Internet: A psychiatrist was walking along a beach in Hawaii when he kicked something in the sand; it was a dusty old bottle. He rubbed it and opened it and out came a genie, who said: "Thank you. I will grant you one wish."

> *I view this honor as a significant sign of how far adoption has come in its journey out of the dark shadows of American culture.*

The psychiatrist considered the offer for a bit and then, laughing, said: "I've always wanted a road from Hawaii to California." The genie grimaced, thought about it a few minutes, then answered: "I'm really sorry, but do you know how much work that would be? Think of all the pilings you'd need to hold up a highway that big, and how long they'd have to be to reach the bottom of the ocean. And all the paving! That's just too much to ask."

The psychiatrist didn't want to be unreasonable, so he said: "Okay. I wish for you to give me insights into my patients, tell me what motivates them to behave as they do, and provide me with answers to their problems. Basically, help me to understand what makes them tick!"

The genie sort of paused, sighed, and said, "Did you want four lanes or eight?"

I am not a genie. Nor am I a psychiatrist or a therapist of any kind. But I think I can help you understand just a little bit about what makes some of your patients tick. More importantly, I hope I can get you all thinking about an array of issues that you might not have considered to a major degree before or factored into your thinking about your professional or personal lives before.

I never gave a second thought to any of the issues I'll discuss tonight until almost a decade ago. That's when I stumbled into the wondrous, little-understood world of adoption for the same reason tens of thousands of people do it every year: my wife, Judy, and I were among those late-blooming baby boomers who waited so long to marry and start a family, we discovered we could no longer do it the old-fashioned way.

It was quite an unnerving jolt when we found out about our infertility, but now we thank God for our corroded plumbing, because—however complicated adoption issues may sometimes be—life without Zack and Emmy would be unbearably empty.

Anyway, once we decided to adopt and began exploring how to do that, we found we knew almost nothing about the process or the institution. In fact, I like to say we knew less than nothing, because most of what we thought we knew was skewed or biased or absolutely wrong.

All of which made our journey more frustrating than it should have been, but it also provided an extraordinary opportunity for me as journalist. It's rare, to say the least, to discover an uncharted planet. But that's what I felt like I'd found.

The short version is that I wound up writing a series of articles for the *Boston Globe*—where I worked for more than 22 years until last June—called "The Adoption Revolution."

The series was well received, including a nomination for a Pulitzer Prize, and it led me to write my book, which tries to deal honestly with a broad spectrum of vexing, gratifying, sometimes strange, and often inspiring issues about which I have come to care more deeply than I do anything other than my own family.

Mostly, I tell stories in my book—personal stories, including my own—that I hope provide insights or perspective into just how profoundly adoption touches even the lives of people who don't realize its impact—which I think includes almost everyone, by the way— and how extensively it really is changing our country.

I discuss those things in broad terms, but I also deal with lots of specific issues relating to the institution and to members of the adoption community. Some are personal issues, such as the normative stages that characterize the development of most adoptees but are generally unrecognized; the unresolved grief that tears at many birth mothers' souls because society allows them so few options or outlets; and the profound insecurities which most adoptive parents confront and which too often lead them to make dubious decisions for themselves and for their children.

Other adoption-related issues I deal with are more policy-oriented. For instance: money's role (which I describe as toxic), and closed records (does everyone know adoptees' records are automatically sealed?), and the revolution in foster care (there's been a record 79 percent increase in adoptions in last five years).

And yet other issues I deal with aren't commonly understood to be adoption-related at all, such as abandoned baby legislation and new reproductive technologies such as donor egg insemination and frozen embryo transfers.

I think one reason we, as a society, have so much trouble dealing with tough questions like these is that we don't understand them in context—as adoption issues, which they absolutely are.

Unfortunately, because they're not viewed that way, we're repeating many of adoption's past mistakes even as adoption is fixing those mistakes for itself. We can talk about this later if you'd like. It's a bit of a digression, but I do want to get people thinking about just how pervasive adoption's role in our country truly is. How pervasive? Eighty to 100 million Americans have adoption in their immediate families. But this is not just about numbers. Let me give you one example: One Chinese girl in an all-white schoolyard—of which there are many all across our country—changes the way all the teachers in that school teach family formation. More fundamentally, that one young person is changing the way all of her classmates—a generation of children—think about nature and nurture, the importance of "blood ties," what constitutes a family, and even what a family looks like. That's quite an impact for just one child, and there are many other comparable examples.

Adoption isn't solely or even principally responsible for the integration into our society of transcultural, multiethnic, multitudinously diverse families headed by infertile couples, straight singles, gay men, lesbians, people with disabilities, and nearly every other sort of parent who never dreamed of being a parent before—or at least couldn't say so out loud or admit who they really were. But I don't think it's too grandiose to say that adoption is contributing, in significant ways, to a historic transformation in both the nature of families and how we all perceive them.

Adoption is contributing, in significant ways, to a historic transformation in both the nature of families and how we all perceive them.

Most people haven't recognized this reality yet, but it's a reality nevertheless. At the same time, I believe we, as a culture and as individuals, also have barely begun to recognize or attempt to correct the negative repercussions of adoption's legacy of secrecy, stigmas, and shame.

Let me give you an example: Every morning, in the newspaper, there's a story about a man who shot his wife and locked his kids in the basement, or some other instance of domestic violence. We don't read that and say: "Oh my God, we can't have biologically formed families. Look what happens!"

Do we learn lessons? Sure, but we don't extrapolate from a single experience and assume we have learned great lessons about an entire institution. But that is what we do with adoption. Fill in the blank in the example I just gave: "adoptive father" shoots wife, etc.

Ah, now we understand, don't we? Well, we understand nothing. But we think we do, because when we have so little real knowledge, we tend to universalize from the small bits of information we receive. It happens that the media—for lots of reasons I can discuss—cover adoption anecdotally, as an aberration, mostly by telling the horror stories, and increasingly, wondrous ones, but not the ones in between the extremes. And that's where real life occurs. So people get their impressions of adoptive life from the aberrations.

That's changing as adoption comes into the light of day. But the results of generations of misinformation and misunderstandings are all around us. And even the words that describe our children— you're adopted—are still sometimes used and perceived as an insult. My children are not an insult. And neither are anyone else's, no matter why they leave a family, how they enter one, or even if they have no family at all.

But we do sometimes think of them that way—not literally, but as somehow less fortunate or even less worthy. And we do sometimes pathologize them, their behaviors, and the institution to which they belong. And I understand why that is: because it's hard to learn about secrets, and we keep secrets about things that we're ashamed of or embarrassed about, right?

So too many of us have come to assume, almost instinctively, that something must be wrong with adoption and its participants. That's reflected in our language and, sometimes, in our behavior. Combined with our general lack of knowledge about the subject, it can sometimes have serious consequences.

Despite all this, most people do think they know a good bit about adoption. But where would they have learned it? Have they read a lot of good books on the subject? Been taught about its realities in school? Social workers get no training in adoption. Neither do teachers or doctors or mental health professionals or journalists.

I am not saying people can't learn on the job, because we obviously do that all the time in all lines of work—and often achieve very good results. But, with minimal formal education and public discussion, we tend to extrapolate from experiences that may or may not be representative and, very often, we try to apply what we incorrectly perceive as similar models to the situation we face at the moment.

The adults and children for whom adoption is an integral part of everyday life are normal people, with normal issues. But their norms are sometimes different. So the teachers, social workers, doctors, therapists, and other professionals who deal with them need to respect and understand the differences.

I'd like to repeat a central point: that adoption is helping to permanently reshape our families and our very understanding of family. Demographers, sociologists, historians, academics, and journalists may not have identified this reality yet, but it's reality nevertheless.

I mean, there are white Americans holding Chinese cultural festivals at synagogues all over America. Is this unprecedented or what? And, for the first time in history, we are changing our country not through an immigrant wave—as we have done in the past—but by bringing in only the children, and their cultures with them. It's a stunning phenomenon that has never transpired anywhere before.

I think most people haven't identified what's happening around us, and to us, for the same reason that Americans' views about adoption remain so full of corrosive stereotypes and basic misconceptions.

That is: This wondrous institution has been a secret for most of history, and it's hard to learn anything about secrets. The first section of my book is called "Don't Whisper, Don't Lie, It's Not a Secret Anymore." Thank God. One of my favorite lines about adoption—though it could apply to virtually any aspect of life—comes from Joyce Maguire Pavao.

Dr. Pavao—who is an adopted person herself—says that "people who grow up with secrets about them think there's something wrong with them."

Everybody's entitled to privacy, and we should always be very careful to remember that as adoption emerges from the hiding phase of its history. But it's time to finally jettison the secrets.

> *To most people, even the word* **adoptee** *conjures mental images and emotional responses relating only to children.*

I don't want to dwell excessively on adoption's problems, and I don't think I do so in my book. I hope, most of the time, we focus on the joys and rewards of family life. But it's also essential we honestly confront the difficulties too, because you can't solve problems that you won't even discuss.

We are obviously doing that now. But until very recently most people in the adoption world didn't talk about the nature of their families at all—ever, at any age—while many children were never told they were adopted. An incredible number of them were told that their biological parents died in car accidents—Harry Potter.

Lies like that have lots of direct negative effects on the people involved, but they also have systemic consequences. It's a good illustration of one of my book's themes: that the policies and attitudes of society as a whole have profound effects on adoption, just as adoption's policies and attitudes have profound effects on society as a whole.

I'll translate into English: as a result of adoption's history of secrecy, for generations most Americans never heard a word their whole lives about the developmental issues, needs, or desires of adoption's participants. They never even knew they came into regular contact with adopted adults, absolutely not birth mothers, and most often not even adoptive parents.

Americans knew there were unmarried women who gave up their babies. And, though they didn't talk about it, they must have understood somebody was adopting those babies. But they never consciously observed those boys and girls growing up. So, to most people, even the word *adoptee* conjures mental images and emotional responses relating only to children.

Adopted adults all know that from personal experience, but most Americans still don't get it. Again, not because they are intellectually deficient or evil, but because it's another legacy of adoption's surreptitious past.

You know, too often when we talk about families—whether there's divorce in them or step-parenting or single parenting or two parents who have different political views or races or religions, or two perfect heterosexual parents who are just trying to live through their children's teenage years—we tend to focus on the issues and problems we confront rather than the joys and rewards we receive.

It makes me feel like a character from one of my favorite jokes. Forgive the ethnic reference; feel free to substitute your own if you retell it; it works just as well. "A waiter walks up to a table full of elderly Jewish couples and says: 'Excuse me. Is anything all right?'"

Well, some things relating to American family life really are all right and others are getting better. Amazingly, for the first time in our history, one of the best and brightest examples is adoption.

Our families are becoming more open, more honest, more healthy and less stigmatized, less pathologized, and less stereotyped. And I believe our progress will accelerate even further as Americans learn more about and from adoption—and, I hope consequently, as they internalize a few basic truths:

That we adoptive parents benefit enormously from having more information about our kids and fewer insecurities about ourselves; that almost no one who creates a life—especially those who nurture it inside of themselves—can then part with the child who emerges and just "move on" as though they've given away an old record player.

And that adoptees—no matter how or why they are placed in new families—love the people who raise them and know they are "real" parents. They do not become ingrates or stalkers or seekers of new mommies and daddies. But they do all grow up, and most want to know—to varying degrees—where, and who, they came from.

I think about adoption in precisely the same way as I do about them. I want my children to be the best I can help to make them. I want them to be ethical, moral, honest, and kind. And those are all the things I want for the institution that allowed Judy and me to become their parents.

Even at this time when we are all consumed by concerns for our personal safety, that still seems like a worthwhile dream. I hope some of you will join me in trying to make it a reality.

Before the States Institute on International Education in the Schools[3]

Rod Paige

Secretary of U.S. Department of Education, 2001– ; born Monticello, MS; bachelor's degree, Jackson State University, Mississippi; master's degree and doctorate, Indiana University; coached in college-level athletics; dean, College of Education, Texas Southern University, establishing that institution's Center for Excellence in Urban Education; trustee and officer, Board of Education, Houston Independent School District (HISD), 1989–94; superintendent of schools, HISD, 1994–2001; chaired Youth Employment Issues Subcommittee, U.S. Department of Labor; member, National Association for the Advancement of Colored People (NAACP); Harold W. McGraw, Jr., Prize in Education, 2000; National Superintendent of the Year by the American Association of School Administrators, 2001.

Editors' introduction: In November 2002 the Asia Society, Council of Chief State School Officers, Education Commission of the States, and National Governors Association co-hosted the first annual States Institute on International Education in the Schools. This event brought together delegations from 22 states, as well as national leaders in policy, business, education, and philanthropy, to explore better ways of preparing U.S. students to be citizens, workers, and leaders in the interconnected world of the 21st century. Secretary Paige told delegates to the institute, "No longer can we afford to focus only on the domestic. Our view must turn more outward toward the world, nurturing relationships with other countries and improving international studies in our schools."

Rod Paige's speach: Thank you, Governor Hunt, for that introduction and for your leadership, along with Governor Engler, on the National Coalition on Asia and International Studies in the Schools.

I thank the National Coalition, the Asia Society, the Council of Chief State School Officers, the Education Commission of the States, and the National Governors Association for your leadership in organizing this institute.

We owe special gratitude to Vivien Stewart of the Asia Society and her staff for all their hard work, as well. And I thank each of you for coming. Your presence here speaks well of your dedication and commitment to the cause of education.

---

3. Delivered on November 20, 2002, at Washington, D.C.

I know it's been a long day and you're all ready for dinner, so I promise to be brief.

I am grateful for this gracious opportunity, because it allows me to share some thoughts during this International Education Week about the role of the Department of Education in the world arena.

We are a domestic agency whose main focus is to ensure that America's public schools provide the best education possible for their students, our country's future leaders.

Our system has drawn many to these shores to learn and to exchange ideas about education. Since becoming secretary of education, I have had the pleasure of meeting many of my counterparts from around the world, along with foreign teachers, journalists, and policy makers. We have formal agreements with about a dozen countries, and we cooperate informally with many more.

This is the way it has gone for the Department of Education since its inception. But on September 11, 2001, the world changed. And our role in it changed.

No longer can we afford to focus only on the domestic. Our view must turn more outward toward the world, nurturing relationships with other countries and improving international studies in our schools.

No longer can we afford to focus only on the domestic. Our view must turn more outward toward the world.

I appreciate this opportunity to announce as part of our acknowledgments of International Education Week, an important policy directive.

ONE: I am directing that the Department of Education broaden its focus and become more engaged in building international relationships through the language of education. For many seeking closer ties with the United States, the Department of Education is a point of entry. We are often approached to develop new relationships, participate in international projects and comparative studies, and brief foreign counterparts on the administration's policies and programs. And we must strengthen and expand these ties.

TWO: I am directing that we expand our efforts to learn from other countries about techniques and practices that will help us improve our own system of education.

THREE: I am directing that we provide leadership on education issues in appropriate international forums and settings, and work with appropriate partners in other countries on initiatives of common benefit.

And FOUR: I am directing that we do a better job of exposing our students in this country to other languages, cultures, and challenges outside our borders.

We already play an important role in developing foreign language and area-studies expertise at the higher education level, through our Fulbright-Hays and Title VI programs. And we will continue. But we need to start that instruction much earlier in our young people's education careers.

As secretary of education, I spend my days working to ensure that every child in America's schools is educated and no child is left behind. That is our mission, and it's a tall order.

Our sweeping new education reforms raised the bar for academic achievement in our public schools, particularly in reading, math, and science. We are working hand in glove with the states to implement these reforms.

We need to put the "world" back into "world-class" education.

But we are ever mindful of the lessons of September 11th that taught us that all future measures of a rigorous K–12 education must include a solid grounding in other cultures, other languages, and other histories.

In other words, we need to put the "world" back into "world-class" education.

Ours is a world of 24-hour-news cycles, global markets, and high-speed Internet. We need look no further than our morning paper to see that our future, and the future of our children, is inextricably linked to the complex challenges of the global community.

And for our children to be prepared to take their place in that world and rise to those challenges, they must first understand it.

Recent studies indicate we have a lot of work to do.

As you know, a study by the Asia Society last year identified a troubling international education gap in America. That study revealed that, although most of us believe our nation's economic future is locked with Asia's, we know very little about this continent where 60 percent of the world's population lives.

Those findings prompted this very conference. And they were more recently reinforced by a disappointing recent snapshot of student geography skills by NAEP—the National Assessment of Educational Progress. NAEP found that 16 percent of 8th graders could not locate the Mississippi River on a map of the United States. And one-third of 4th graders could not identify the state where they live. The state where they live.

More of the same came out in a report released just this morning by the National Geographic Society. That report showed that young American adults lag far behind their global counterparts in current events and geographic literacy. Among the findings were these:

Despite the ongoing conflict in the Middle East and the terrorist attack on America, 83 percent of young Americans surveyed could not find Afghanistan on a map. More Americans knew the correct location of the TV show *Survivor*, which was in the South Pacific, than knew how to find Israel. When young adults from nine countries, including those in Europe, Japan, and Mexico, were asked which country served as the base for the Taliban and Al Qaeda, young Americans came in last with the correct answer: Afghanistan.

Clearly, to meet our goal to leave no child behind, we must shift our focus from current practice and encourage programs that introduce our students to international studies earlier in their education, starting in kindergarten.

I will seek legislative authority, or build on existing authority, to support international education in our K–12 schools through partnerships with local colleges and universities.

International content can be integrated into the teaching of many subjects.

I will also work to partner with states to provide new resources in support of high-quality K–12 programs that provide international knowledge and skills in our nation's classrooms.

International education shouldn't be an add-on. International content can be integrated into the teaching of many subjects. When children read stories, some should be by and about people in other countries. Students in dual language immersion programs often study some of their math, science, and other lessons in that language. They are building skills in both English and another language at the same time that they are learning subject-matter content. Some children in our country are learning these skills, but many more could and should do it.

And starting this year, the department will each year recognize a teacher whose outstanding work has helped our young people understand world issues and other countries, cultures, and languages.

Next year during International Education Week, I hope to meet that outstanding teacher.

These proposals will build upon international outreach already under way at the department, in program areas including special education, postsecondary education, education statistics, federal student aid, school safety, and many others.

Our Migrant Education program works throughout the year with migrant education officials in U.S. states, Mexican states, and the federal government of Mexico to help ensure that no child is left behind because his or her parents are agricultural workers who migrate across borders to earn a living.

We are working with other countries, such as in the U.S.–China eLanguage project, which aims to provide opportunities to learn English and Chinese to people in both countries using the Internet.

This is the start of providing opportunities for students to learn languages on-line through authentic situations so that they are not prevented from learning a second or third language by the shortage of foreign-language teachers.

A year ago, President Bush and I unveiled the Friendship Through Education initiative to help children and schools in Afghanistan. In response, American students reached out to share their thoughts, their dreams, and their culture with students in Afghanistan refugee camps and other countries in the Middle, Far, and Near East.

And in the exchange, many found they are more alike than different.

Not only do programs such as this promote a greater understanding of people halfway around the world, they also reinforce that while we may differ in our language, our worship, and our traditions, we all share a common desire: to learn.

Education lifts all people and all societies. It is as fundamental a human right as the right to breathe.

In that spirit, the president's decision to rejoin UNESCO is a major step forward. And I assure you that the Department of Education will be a strong and constructive partner with UNESCO in its efforts to advance the cause of education to all reaches of the earth.

I have conveyed our department's enthusiastic support of the re-entry to UNESCO to Director-General Matsuura and to the Secretary-General Kofi Annan. And we are already working with the Department of State to move forward.

In that spirit of our new policy, tomorrow morning, the Department of Education and the government of the United Kingdom will open a dialogue on "A New Vision of Citizenship."

Over the next two days here in Washington, policymakers and practitioners from both countries will talk about ways to encourage young people to become engaged and make a difference in their communities.

This weekend, I will travel to Mexico, along with Secretary Powell and other cabinet secretaries, for the annual meeting of our two governments, the U.S.–Mexico Binational Commission.

I will be meeting with my counterpart, Education Secretary Reyes Tamez, and his team to talk about how we can strengthen our work together in areas like migrant education, English and Spanish language acquisition, teacher exchanges, distance education, special education, and higher education.

We will report on our progress to President Fox. As with many countries, education is an important part of our relationship with Mexico.

The Department of Education is taking the international lead that the world of the 21st century demands of us. And I want to hear from you. You are on the front lines, so we welcome your input and advice.

We believe that what you are setting out to do is among the most important tasks for educators, and for all of us, in the coming years.

Thank you.

Opening Remarks to National Conference "Children 2003, Imagine an America"[4]

Shay Bilchik

President and CEO, Child Welfare League of America (CWLA), 2000– ; B.S. (1975) and J.D. (1977), University of Florida; assistant state attorney, 11th Judicial Circuit of Florida, Miami, 1977–93; associate deputy attorney general, Department of Justice, 1993–94; administrator, Office of Juvenile Justice and Delinquency Prevention (OJJDP), the U.S. Department of Justice, 1994–2000; chairs Maryland's State Advisory Board on Juvenile Justice.

Editors' introduction: Based in Washington, D.C., the Child Welfare League of America, with nearly 1,200 member agencies nationwide, is the oldest and largest national nonprofit organization developing and promoting policies and programs to protect America's children while strengthening America's families. In his addresses, as in this one before an audience of about 1,500 at the annual National Conference of the Child Welfare League of America, President Bilchik carries the message that children must be made a priority in society. As he reminds those gathered, "Investments in children always grow," and with children rest "our best hopes for the improvement of the human condition."

Shay Bilchik's speech: Thank you, Ray, for that generous introduction. Let me officially welcome you all to *Children 2003, Imagine an America*.

Imagine an America where every child is healthy, safe, and thriving, and where all children develop to their full potential.

These ringing words, which you saw on the cover of your conference program and will be seeing and hearing around you throughout the week, are, as you know, the opening words of *Making Children a National Priority: A Framework for Community Action*. They are an invitation to consider what might be, and what ought to be, instead of what is. Many young people *do* succeed, and many excellent programs engage communities in nurturing their potential—but we are not yet reaching far enough—perhaps because our imaginings have not been sufficiently bold, and inclusive, until now.

---

4. Delivered on March 5, 2003, at Washington, D.C. Reprinted with permission of Shay Bilchik.

We find ourselves at an historical moment when our nation and its citizens are strongly focused on safety and protection.

Fear, if we give in to it, tends to draw us into ourselves and make us think small.

At the same time, the Child Welfare League of America, through our Framework for Community Action, is challenging us all to think generously and expansively . . . to ground ourselves in hope instead of fear . . . to imagine, and then to realize an America where all children are safe, healthy, and thriving.

We cannot wish away the negatives. In the course of this hard winter, some among us have gone beyond cocooning to bunkering, giving in to an impulse to think small and to avoid risks. Yet, during tough times we need each other more, not less. We need more collaboration, not more competition. We need more reaching out, not more pulling in. We need more creativity, not more hanging on to old ways that may no longer work.

We need to acknowledge the reality of the fear and concern that have motivated many official decisions since September of 2001, as well as the harsh economic climate that seems to narrow all our horizons. But at the same time—now more than ever—we need to let our hopes and our imaginations soar. *We have to take care of our children.* We have to make America's children a national priority. Are you with me?!

So how are we doing, as a nation, at caring for our children? In the world at large, according to statistics from the Children's Defense Fund, the United States is:

- 1st in military technology,
- 1st in Gross National Product, and
- 1st in health technology,
- but 22nd in preventing infant mortality and
- last—I could say dead last—in protecting children against gun violence.

The sad fact is that we failed to raise the quality of life for many American families during the fat years of the '90s, and now that the years are lean, too many families are still falling behind.

- 12 million children in America live in poverty.
- In 2002, requests for emergency food and shelter assistance rose 20 percent over the previous year.

And we know that when families are stressed by anxiety about meeting their basic needs, the incidence of child neglect and abuse increases.

- The number of children reported for abuse and neglect hovered right below 3 million in 2000, and we are hearing from many states that when the statistics are finally available, we will likely see climbing numbers for the past two years.

- And every day in America three children died of abuse or neglect in the year 2000—a total of 1,236. Please, visualize that number: it is 40 classrooms, with 30 children in each, who are murdered as a result of child abuse in one year.

Now we all know that responsibility for our children's safety and well-being resides with many people, beginning with parents and kin, and reaching outward to friends and neighbors, to professionals such as teachers, child care providers, police officers, social workers, and foster parents, and up to the highest government officials. We're interested, though, in fixing the problems, not in fixing the blame.

That's what we're here at this conference to do. It's an opportunity, throughout these three days, to learn from your peers, in child welfare and other systems, about all the ways we can work harder, and smarter, and more collaboratively, to secure better outcomes for kids. It's an opportunity to celebrate good people in other sectors, like the corporate and foundation world, who help us to do our work. We'll be recognizing Prudential Financial and five other corporations Thursday evening, and the Freddie Mac Foundation on Friday. And it's an opportunity, especially tomorrow, to tell our representatives on Capital Hill that we cannot continue to do the work we do, and see the outcomes we want to see, without stronger—perhaps more creative—but also stronger, federal support.

> *Imagine what this great nation could accomplish, if the well-being of all children was truly a national priority.*

We are doing everything we can, as one organization with a growing network of partnerships, to provide the knowledge child welfare professionals need to apply evidence-based, reliable solutions. But to realize our vision for the children of this nation, will take more than professionals. Imagine what our schools and neighborhoods and cities would look like—imagine what this great nation could accomplish, if the well-being of *all* children was truly a national priority. Imagine what could happen if parents, kin, professionals, citizens, and governments worked together to support and strengthen *all* children and families!

The Framework is CWLA's invitation to imagine that America and make it real. Through the Framework for Community Action, CWLA organizes our program, policy, advocacy, membership, training, and consultation resources to work in partnership with parents, communities, and professionals to realize the vision.

The core of the Framework, the foundation on which it rests, is a statement of the five universal needs of children. They are:

"The Basics": At the most fundamental level, children need proper nutrition, economic security, adequate shelter and clothing, education, and primary and preventive health and mental health care. And those needs also include—

Relationships: Children need close, nurturing relationships with parents, kin, and other caregivers; caring relationships with community members, including neighbors, coaches, teachers, and faith community leaders and members; and good relationships with siblings and peers. They need—

Opportunities: Yes, children and youth need opportunities to develop their talents and skills, to contribute to their families and communities, and to make positive connections to their cultures, traditions, and spiritual resources. And our children need—

Safety: Children need to be kept safe from abuse and neglect by their caregivers, as well as from witnessing or being victimized by family, school, or community violence. Children also need to be safe from discrimination, media violence, Internet victimization, environmental toxins, and accidental injury. And fifth, children need healing.

Healing: When we are unable to protect children, we must do all that we can to ease the impact of the harm they have suffered. Helping children and youth to heal involves ensuring their immediate and ongoing safety, supplying immediate and continuing emotional support, assessing the need for and providing medical, mental health, and other needed services, and, in some cases, making amends through restorative justice practices.

Every child and every youth has these same needs, whether they live on a farm, in the inner city, or in a suburban tract home . . . in a mansion, in a ghetto, in a foster home, a group home, or a juvenile detention facility. Yet, we, as a nation, do not meet these needs for hundreds of thousands of children and youth, especially poor children, children of color, and, too often, children in our "systems." If you think about it, all of the workshops at this conference address meeting children's needs.

People who care about children *can* collaborate across systems. We *can* work smarter, and sometimes we can rearrange the funding streams to make systems work better for families and kids, in ways that respect their dignity and draw on their inherent strengths. But when you see what we are able to accomplish, it only makes you marvel at what we could do if we weren't trying to build bricks with straw.

Imagine an America in which successful, tested programs are systematically and methodically taken to scale, instead of being allowed to wither because the grant ran out or the charismatic leader moved into retirement. Imagine!!!

We know it can happen, because it is already happening in pockets of excellence around the U.S. But this is such an enormous country, that many children, young people, and families still struggle alone. Imagine a time when a child's well-being does not depend on an accident of geography. Imagine that America!!!

The United States of America can afford to meet the needs of all America's children.

Albert Einstein said that "imagination is more important than knowledge." I believe we need both. CWLA's Framework team has collected many examples of successful community collaboration for its first Community Implementation Guide. Our Research to Practice team collects examples of promising practices in specific programmatic areas, so we can lift them up as models for replication or adaptation nationwide. We are convinced that for every challenge, somewhere in this vast, resourceful, and caring nation, an effective solution is in place.

Ladies and gentlemen, this is the wealthiest and most powerful nation the world has ever known. Its citizens are a vast reservoir of talent and imagination and goodwill. The United States of America can afford to meet the needs of all America's children. People in communities across the country can meet these needs for all of their children.

It won't happen all at once, and it won't happen quickly. We must think comprehensively and inclusively across systems. We must begin in each community with a candid assessment of our children's well-being—both strengths and shortcomings; a vision for their future that is shared by all the necessary community stakeholders; a thoughtful, realistic plan built on what we know works; and the resources, talents, energy, commitment, and hard work of many people to make that vision a reality.

On a small scale, it is happening already. Let me tell you about one of the real-life programs that we have identified in the Framework and its Community Implementation Guide:

At least 8 million U.S. children—that would be approximately 12 percent of all children—and as many as 11 million, a number I heard more recently—lack health and mental health insurance coverage. This means that their families rely on hospital emergency rooms, and receive little or no primary or preventive care.[1]

Colorado has taken a unique, cross-disciplinary approach to addressing children's mental health needs. An early intervention pilot supported by the Colorado General Assembly puts early childhood mental health specialists on site at child care and Head Start sites. Results from the pilot sites showed fewer childhood expulsions (Imagine being expelled from preschool! Sadly, it happens all the time.) and better capacity to manage challenging behavior on the part of teachers and assistants.

Other good examples are out there, across America, and CWLA staff members are hard at work researching them and documenting them. I am grateful to those of you who sent in program ideas for the Community Implementation Guide. We expect this upcoming volume, available in June, to be the first of a series. It will offer practical tools and resources that communities can use to support families and children.

We anticipate that communities will use the Framework to guide assessment and to anchor planning for both new and existing community change efforts, as at least one community already has, and that each successful implementation will seed others.

Workshop E-5, on Friday morning, will focus on the upcoming Framework Community Implementation Guide. Workshop F-5, also on Friday morning, will address how a group of rural Oklahoma counties used the five universal needs as a framework in their planning efforts.

Let me pause, before I go any further, to honor a person who is no longer with us. Rosie Oreskovich was the very dedicated and effective assistant secretary of the Children's Administration in Washington State. Under her leadership, DSHS devised and implemented a transformative *Kids Come First Agenda*. Since the news of her passing arrived late last week, those who loved her have been celebrating her legacy. Rosie accomplished more than most people do in longer lifetimes. But I know that if she were here now she would tell you about the work that remains undone, and she would challenge us all to carry it forward. Rosie always put children and families first. Her loss is a blow to us all—but also an opportunity for re-commitment.

Ladies and gentlemen, we each have choices to make. We can choose to feel victimized and to become immobilized by our worries. But, "worry is a misuse of the imagination." OR, we can choose to act with courage, to move out of our comfort zones and experiment with new thinking and new actions.

Children are not quite 26 percent of our U.S. population, but they are 100 percent of our future. Investing in helping *all* children grow into caring and competent adults is investing in our future. Please tell those people on Capitol Hill and back at home: *Investments in children always grow.* Tell everyone you know.

To fail to invest in our children—or worse yet, to disinvest, or to accept the status quo—would be to break faith with our future, with our best hopes for the improvement of the human condition. I imagine something far better, and I know you do too.

Note

1. CPS Annual Demographic Survey, March Supplement. *http://www.ferret.bls.census.gov/macro/032002/health/h08_000.htm.*

Real Life Unplugged[5]

Karen E. Dill

Associate professor of psychology, Lenoir-Rhyne College, Hickory, NC, 1997– ; born St. Louis, MO, November 19, 1969; A.B. (1991), M.A. (1994), and Ph.D. (1997) in psychology, University of Missouri; recent work on violent video games has received worldwide interest, including interviews by Time, CNN, *and* ABC News; *testified before Congress for the American Psychological Association about the influence of violent video games on children's health; has led media literacy workshops; co-authored "Effects of Aggressive Personality on Social Expectations and Social Perceptions" (with Anderson, Anderson, and Deuser), 1997, nominated for article of the year by the* Journal of Research in Personality.

Editors' introduction: Dr. Dill, a social psychologist, has recently investigated the effects of violent video games upon children. In addressing some 120 persons attending the regular meeting of the Rotary Club in Hickory, NC, she concluded that, "Playing a lot of violent video games teaches kids . . . that violence is appropriate, rewarding, effective, and without negative consequences." Professor Dill recalled one "humorous" aspect of the meeting: "I entitled my speech, 'Real Life Unplugged,' and when Mr. David B. Myers, president of the club, started to introduce me, his microphone suddenly popped and went dead. I thought that was an omen."

Karen E. Dill's speech: I've given a lot of speeches lately. I've spoken to seventh graders, high schoolers, parents, college seniors, and prospective college students. Most often I have spoken about media violence and related issues—which I am going to get to today. However, when I sat down to collect my thoughts and decide what I was going to say to you all today, I asked myself a question that I think all speech writers should ask. And that question is, "What do I have to say?"

I have the same philosophy with giving speeches as I do when I teach my classes, and that is that when I talk, it is not merely to hear the sound of my voice, which I frankly don't find that entertaining, but it is to communicate something. Something real. Something worth talking about.

---

5. Delivered on March 6, 2003, at noon, at the Lake Hickory Country Club, Hickory, NC. Reprinted with permission of Karen E. Dill.

I knew I had something to say, but I wasn't sure exactly where I was going to go with this speech until yesterday. Yesterday morning, for two hours, I had 16 teenagers in my house. These were my students from my honors General Psychology class.

In the class, in addition to reading a standard General Psychology textbook, we read a book about creativity. Maybe you've heard of the book, it's called *A Whack on the Side of the Head*, by Roger Von Oech. The premise of the book is that many of us stifle our own creativity because we fall victim to what Von Oech calls, "Mental Locks" or barriers to creativity that we think are there but are really just our perceptions. The mental locks include the simple but powerful belief that we are not creative, the fear of getting out of our own area of expertise, the desire to avoid looking foolish, and the idea that play is frivolous. Once you get past these mental locks, you open the door to creativity. Sometimes, according to Von Oech, we need "A Whack on the Side of the Head," to clear our mind of these artificial constraints.

Let me share with you one story that Von Oech relates in *A Whack on the Side of the Head*. The story involves what he calls, "The Aslan Phenomenon." It seems that Von Oech's neighbor had a dog named Aslan that he liked very much. He liked him so much that when he would take his morning run, he purposefully ran by Aslan's house, so he could stop and pet the dog. Years later, after Aslan no longer lived in his neighborhood, Von Oech realized that he was still running the same way, but no longer had a reason for doing so. The moral of the story: Sometimes decisions that used to make sense no longer do because the situation changes. Von Oech reminds us that, "No one likes change, except a wet baby." Even so, change happens around us whether we like it or not, and it's up to us to be thoughtful and notice the change, and then adapt to that change.

Because the topic of creativity was a focus of my honors General Psychology course, I asked each student to do a creative project of his or her choosing. Yesterday was the day they came to my house and presented their creative projects to the class. For two hours I watched in awe as these young people presented their work. One student had taught himself to play the guitar, and he played and sang for us. Another created a wire sculpture. It was a globe and the globe was formed of six intertwined wire people. She said the theme of the sculpture was global unity. Another student had written a Christian song. He brought along two of his friends from the dorm who accompanied him on their guitars and sang. A young woman had mapped her family tree. She wanted to learn more about her family, and she included long, funny letters from her grandmother who had told her anecdotes about her German ancestors, whom she had never met.

I learned that one of my students was a clog dancer and had taught another student to clog dance. In my front driveway, with a country crooner in the background singing, "I like it, I love it, I want some more of it," my two students clog danced their hearts out. This fact, by the way, was not lost on my neighbors, who witnessed it from their windows.

Now you might be wondering at this point how this relates to video games or to the media at all. Well, I promise I'm going to get there.

Playing a lot of violent video games teaches kids violence.

I am a social psychologist and I've done research on aggression, video game violence, and on how women and minorities are portrayed in video games. What I've found in all this research can really be boiled down to a simple phrase: "Garbage in, garbage out."

Playing a lot of violent video games teaches kids violence. There are many reasons for this. The military uses violent video games to train aggression because the games are killing simulators. Unfortunately in this case, practice is a powerful teaching tool. Violent video games teach kids that violence is appropriate, rewarding, effective, and without negative consequences. The sacred nature of life is perverted into nonexistence.

Other forms of media such as television and movies often teach such antisocial lessons as well. These forms of media, by and large, glorify violence, casual sex, and consumerism.

I would argue that the media, whether it be video games, television, or the Internet, has too often taken the place of what I would call "real life." On a yearly basis, kids spend more time watching TV than they spend in school. Watching TV is the number one waking activity of kids, and it is quickly being joined in popularity by video game playing and Internet surfing.

Not only are the messages in the media typically antisocial, with the average 18 year old witnessing over 200,000 acts of televised violence in their lifetimes, but what's also crucial to understand is that media addiction is also important in that it displaces other activities. Research shows that when people consume more media, they are more likely to do poorly in school, to be poor readers, to have impaired social skills, lower quality time with their family, and to be obese. Kids spend about 28 hours a week watching TV and about a half an hour talking to their dad. The television is on for 7 hours and 40 minutes a day in the average household, and individual family members typically watch different programs in different rooms. 40 percent of U.S. households report watching TV during dinner.

There are many issues here, all of which I would greatly enjoy discussing, but because of time constraints I will focus on one today. There is a national organization called TV Turnoff network, which sponsors a national TV Turnoff Week each spring. This year it is from April 21–27th. I am helping to organize, here in Hickory, a local TV Turnoff Week. For one week, kids and parents pledge to watch no television and play no video games. One thing that has surprised me greatly as I've made plans for this year's TV Turnoff Week is that kids simply don't know what they would do if they did turn off the media. The national organization includes suggestions to tell the kids for "TV Free" activities. These include writing a story, washing the dog, riding a bike, and climbing a tree.

The fact that the kids truly don't know what to do if they are not watching TV amazes me, and I think it's an important point. People my age and older might not be aware of this mentality. I know when I was growing up, our television simply carried three local networks. We did not have cable, the Internet, or even a VCR, so consequently I did not grow up in a media-saturated environment like our kids do today.

I want you to think about something. Think about a moment from your life when you felt happy to be alive. Think about a time when you felt fulfilled as a person, a time when you felt joy, one of those times you will never forget. At the end of your life, you could look back on this moment and count it as one of your favorites. Okay, take a moment to think of that memory. . . . Now let me ask you a question. How many people here remembered a time when you were watching TV, playing a video game, or surfing the Internet? It's a ridiculous question, right? But many people today spend the great majority of their lives doing three basic things: 1) working, 2) necessary functions like eating and sleeping, and 3) watching TV or other media. Is that real life? Is that living? For how many households in America do you think this is true? It's true for the majority of Americans.

So why did I tell you today about my students' creative projects? I told you about them because it reminded me of the simple joy of being a human being. The creative act is meaningful. Sharing your experiences with other people is meaningful. Sitting in front of the TV or video game terminal for hours a day wastes precious time that could be spent really living. It's easy to get caught up in a rut of media use and not realize it.

Maybe we need "A Whack on the Side of the Head" to get us out of that media rut.

Do you have kids who are spending most of their time plugged into media and unplugged from life? How about grandkids? How about you yourself? If so, then I encourage you to try something different. Write a song, trace your family tree . . . clog dance in the front yard if you want to. I know you won't regret it. And I know that years from now, it will be much more memorable than watching another tired episode of the latest sitcom.

And if anyone would like to get involved in this year's TV Turnoff Week, or knows someone who might, please let me know. I'd love to talk to you about it.

Thank you for your time and attention. Now get out there and clog dance!

Meeting of the African American Heritage Parade Committee[6]

Gwendolyn L. Harris

Commissioner, New Jersey Department of Human Services, 2002– ; born Hartford, CT, October 16, 1950; B.A., University of Connecticut, 1972; master's degree, School of Social Service Administration, University of Chicago, 1974; currently pursuing Ph.D. in urban planning and policy development, Bloustein School of Planning and Public Policy, Rutgers University; Community Mental Health Center, College of Medicine and Dentistry of New Jersey, Newark, NJ, 1974–77; director, Social Services, Independence High School, Newark, NJ, 1977–78; founder and executive director, Newark Emergency Services for Families, 1979–80; district office manager and assistant regional administrator, New Jersey Division of Youth and Family Services, 1980–88; program director, New Community Corporation, Newark, NJ, 1988–90; director, Trenton's Department of Health and Human Services, 1990–95; chief of staff to Trenton's Mayor Douglas H. Palmer, 1996–2002; Equal Justice Medal, Legal Services of New Jersey, 1998; Ethel Downing Johnson Memorial Award, Trenton, NJ, YWCA, 1999; Public Policy Leadership Award from Rutgers University School of Social Work, 2003.

Editors' introduction: The New Jersey Department of Human Services (DHS) serves more than one million of the state's most vulnerable citizens and comprises about one-quarter of the state's workforce and budget, with more than 19,000 employees. As has occurred with many states over the years, New Jersey experienced a tragedy in 2003 that led citizens and organizations to debate how better to care for neglected children. In this case, Tyrone Williams, 4, and Raheem Williams, 7, were found malnourished and neglected, and their brother Faheem Williams deceased, while their mother was incarcerated. After an inquiry by the National Association of Social Workers of New Jersey and others, New Jersey lawmakers proposed legislation requiring the state to care for a child whose sole caretaker is incarcerated. In her speech, Commissioner Harris stressed "the public health crisis we are facing—our black children dying at the hands of those who care for them." She asked that citizens once again be "their brother's keeper."

---

6. Delivered on April 19, 2003, at Newark, NJ.

Gwendolyn L. Harris's speech: Thank you, Jeannine, for that kind introduction. I am honored by the invitation from the African American Heritage Parade Committee to be your speaker this morning. This is an organization for which I have a great deal of respect. Your efforts have not only impacted African Americans in the city of Newark, but throughout the state.

In addressing your theme of holistic health . . . I am going to take a broader approach and talk about the health of our community and our families.

I want to focus on the public health crisis we are facing—our black children dying at the hands of those who care for them.

We come together this morning to celebrate our African American heritage, and I have no doubt that most of us have witnessed first-hand and enjoyed significant gains made possible by our ancestors:

- The black middle class and home ownership has reached an all time high.

- The number of African Americans with advanced degrees has increased and continues to rise.

- Our employment options have expanded; we are no longer limited to positions of unskilled labor or as domestic servants—in fact, the largest department in New Jersey state government, with a budget of $8.5 billion and 20,000 employees, is headed by a black woman for the first time in history.

Indeed, we have much to celebrate. But as we celebrate what is good among us, we must also acknowledge what is wrong.

For some us, these are the best of times. But for others, it may very well be the worst of all times—particularly for our children. Do you realize that over 40 percent of the child deaths due to abuse or neglect in this state last year were African American children?

It has been said that in order for us to understand where we are going we must understand where we have been. I believe that this applies to the crisis we are now facing with our families and children. As we celebrate our heritage we must look to it to provide us direction and strength to address today's crisis.

We have a crisis today because far too many of our children are starving, literally—starving for safety, starving for nurturance.

How is it that with *all* of the gains and successes made possible by our ancestors, that our children are being robbed of their hopes and dreams and their very lives?

They are: home alone, beaten, bruised, neglected, lost to parents on drugs, lost to parents who can't parent, and lost to parents who have given up on themselves and therefore have nothing left to give to their children.

If life is like a baseball game, then our families are the farm teams that prepare us for the big leagues. Our children need healthy, stable, strong families to prepare them for life.

It seems to me that there was a time in the black community when the family was just that. It instilled self-reliance and prepared us for the big terrible world outside.

Even during slavery when our relatives were sold, chased off, or taken away to war we fought to stay together and to organize ourselves into family structures. That is how we survived!

When circumstances arose, and children were left unprotected by their own parents, they were still *our* children, and we took those children in, even if they were not part of our bloodline. The extended family has always been a part of our reality. We protected our young from the outside world until the day when *they* had to face it; we *prepared* our young to take the world's responsibilities on and to *succeed*, when that day came—to succeed as members of the community, and as parents.

But today our babies are dying in their own homes and at the hand of those who should be protecting them. Eleven of the twenty-four children who died last year from abuse or neglect in New Jersey were African American. That is 46 percent! African Americans are not 46 percent of the New Jersey population. Almost 50 percent of the child deaths so far this year due to abuse or neglect are African American. Why is this happening?

And to bring it home, 16 percent of all child deaths from abuse or neglect reported during the years of 1998–2002 occurred right here in the city of Newark, 25 percent in 2002 alone. My fear is that in Newark this crisis is getting even worse.

So far this year—from January to April 17th—eleven children have died from abuse or neglect and five of those deaths were African American children. Three of the eleven deaths occurred right here in Newark. What's up with this?

Indeed I am not bringing this to your attention to shock or to shame, I just believe that unless we as a family share the truth and acknowledge the problem—we will not solve the problem.

I also want to say that Mayor Sharpe James and I met some weeks ago and committed to work together to do what government can and must to respond to this crisis.

I contend nevertheless that the black family and the black community consist of more than just government. Our history has taught us that it is only when we, as a people, take responsibility for our *own* destiny that we have been *able* to make *significant* strides forward. That is how we got the right to vote. That is how we were able eat in the restaurant our money could afford, or sit in the seat on the bus or train that was available and suited us.

I am not saying that government does not have a responsibility— and I truly believe and commit to my piece of government getting much better at protecting our children.

But I want to focus today on our collective responsibility to our family and our children. What has gone wrong? We are killing off our young. Or standing by allowing it to happen.

And please don't say it's poverty. My parents told me about poverty, and I am clear that poverty is not an excuse for lack of pride, lack of cleanliness, or lack of the will to succeed. Poverty is not an excuse to kill off our young.

Our people survived Jim Crow, the depression, two world wars, and the civil rights era with a whole lot of pride and willpower and very little money. But we survived.

We were self-reliant, and our families buoyed our efforts.

So what is wrong with us now? I have two thoughts.

There is this me, myself, and I mentality that is *so* powerfully destructive. I am no longer my brother's keeper—that's somebody else's job; that's the government's responsibility. All *I* can concern *myself* with is figuring out a way to succeed for *my* nuclear family and *myself*. I won't associate with anyone who can't help *me*. . . . This is not consistent with *our African* heritage—the sense that we are all interconnected and responsible for one another.

My other thought is that we don't find it fashionable to talk about

---

While the family, **as** *an institution, is under tremendous strain, the fact is that in black America the family tends to suffer from these pressures even greater.*

---

values these days. We don't *talk* about what we believe in! Whether it be the Ten Commandments or the Nguzo Saba—we aren't sharing what we believe in, right and wrong, good and bad. Our community has taken a live and let live position that really translates into live and let our children die.

While the family, *as* an institution, is under tremendous strain, the fact is that in black America the family tends to suffer from these pressures even greater. Saving our families, especially our children, is going to take *all* of us stepping up to the plate and doing our part.

We must be prepared to say unequivocally what we believe in; what is right and what is wrong; what is good and what is unacceptable. Thou shall not steal or bear false witness or covet. Honor thy mother and thy father. Keeping silent about what we believe gives tacit approval for what is wrong.

We must be prepared to teach and to love—and not just our own children, but also our neighbor's child. We can't just save our own child; we have to save the child across town too, because their worlds are inextricably intertwined. And *we* may be their *last* hope to learn right from wrong, to *learn* collective work and responsibility, faith or purpose.

We all have the capacity and more importantly, the responsibility to nurture families to help them be healthy and secure. We all have an obligation to think more about what we put in the hearts and minds of the children we create and the children we come into contact with.

We also have an obligation to help the parents that we come in contact with. There are many in our community who are *simply* not prepared to be parents.

Share with them what they may not know:

- Babies *should* be placed to sleep on their back, back to sleep (SIDS deaths).

- They should not share their bed with their baby (roll over deaths).

- A baby or toddler should never be left unattended for even one minute in bath water.

- Evaluate who you leave your child with, even for just a couple of hours.

- And for God's sake *never*, *ever* shake a baby or a small child (shaken baby syndrome).

We need to teach all parents that all children need to be:

- protected and comforted

- kept clean

- talked to with a kind voice

- cared for when sick

- immunized

- born free of drugs

We need to help them to understand that from the minute a child is born, his or her brain is shaped by what they experience.

Let them know that as parents they are the most important people in their child's life and their children will *learn* from them *how* to treat others.

As a community we must acknowledge that

- Right here in New Jersey there are 6,931 children in foster care and over 4,500 are African American.

- Of the children awaiting adoption through DYFS, the majority of them are older African American boys.

- Eighty-six percent of the poorest children in New Jersey do not live with a father and over half have no contact with him.

These are indicators of our troubled families—and the *work we* have before *us* to strengthen our families and to *save* our children.

I challenge you this morning to think of what *you* can do to address the needs of our children.

When I grew up, I was encompassed by a triangle of love, as I'm sure most of you were. That triangle was comprised of home, church, and school. This is what lifted me and my peers up, and caught us when we fell.

But today points of that triangle are weakened. So in our commitment to rebuild our families, we must require our churches, community groups, and civic associations to play the *active* role they once did in saving our young.

I share with you an African proverb that speaks volumes to me: "The ruin of a nation begins in the homes of its people."

This suggests to me that we must begin seeking a change from within and among ourselves, beginning in our homes, with our families—or we will all be ruined.

We must show our young that they are worthy of love. We must give them something to believe in, values, a sense of right and wrong, good and bad, such that they can grow to be productive citizens and nurturing, effective parents.

In the African American family, we value our children. This is *our* heritage. Therefore, we need to protect our children. They are our legacy.

No people can survive if they kill off their young—*or* if they just stand by and let their young die.

Let us pledge to do this in the *name* of our children.

I offer the name of Faheem Williams.

Unfortunately, I can offer some others as well.

I can offer the names of:

Tasha
And Destiny
And Tasheer
And Marco
And Isaiah
And Nakaya
And Kushann
And Brian
And Baby Boy Morris
And Josette

These children all lived and died here in Essex County at the hand of those charged with their care—from child abuse or neglect.

Think about that for a minute.

And then, let us all resolve to do *all* that we can.

We must put our children first, for they are our future.

Let's wrap our arms around our children, protect them, nurture them—and lift them up.

That is what our ancestors did for us, and that is what we must do for our children today.

Thank you.

V. The Spirit of Adventure

Creating a Better Future[1]

Joseph Bordogna

Deputy director and chief operating officer, National Science Foundation, 1999– ; born Scranton, PA, March 22, 1933; B.S. (1955) and Ph.D. (1964) in electrical engineering, University of Pennsylvania; RCA Corp., 1958–64; assistant, associate, then full professor, University of Pennsylvania, 1964– ; associate dean of engineering and applied science, 1973–80, acting dean, 1980–81, and dean, 1981–90; director, Moore School of Electrical Engineering, 1976–90; with National Science Foundation: director of engineering (1991–96) and acting deputy director (1996–99); author Electric Networks *(with H. Ruston, 1966) and* The Man Made World *(with others, 1971); several awards for engineering, including Modernization Leadership Award, National Coalition for Advanced Manufacturing, 1993, induction into Engineering Educators Hall of Fame, 1993, and chairman's award, American Association of Engineering Societies, 1994.*

Editors' introduction: With young American soldiers stationed throughout the world from Bosnia to Afghanistan, armed conflict continuing in the Middle East, and large companies eliminating jobs through restructuring, people graduating from college in 2002 faced an uncertain future. In addressing graduates at the University of Maryland Baltimore County (UMBC) Graduate School commencement, Dr. Bordogna encouraged them to be innovative and to *"challenge the world you're given."* Then, he continued, "you may discover that it's not just the world you transform in the process, but yourselves as well."

Joseph Bordogna's speech: Thank you, Dr. Hrabowski. And good morning to you all. I am honored and delighted to be a part of this University of Maryland, Baltimore County commencement. I admire the energy and spirit that are so much a part of the UMBC environment. This is a university that is going places: united, motivated, bold, courageous!

And you, graduates of the Class of 2002, are in the vanguard. Congratulations to all of you, and to your families and friends. This is a time to celebrate your success and to take pride in your accomplishments.

---

1. Delivered on May 22, 2002, at 10:00 A.M. in the Retriever Activities Center at Baltimore, MD. Reprinted with permission of Joseph Bordogna.

It's appropriate to pause at this important milestone in your lives to refresh yourselves and refocus your energies on what lies ahead. I can already anticipate a future in which you will make your unique and collective contributions in serving and leading this nation.

It's my job today to provide something useful for the unknown ahead—and to be brief about it!

Believe it or not, I can remember very clearly my own commencement. I come from a large family—birth and foster—and *all* of them attended my graduation. My relatives made quite a crowd that day. I was the first in my family to graduate from college, so when my moment of glory came and I walked up the aisle to receive my diploma, they all beamed with pride as they shared our joint accomplishment. It was their moment of glory, too. I'll never forget it! I'm positive that today will be as memorable in *your* lives.

In this greater sense of commonweal, each of you shares an exceptional kinship on this occasion not only with immediate family, but with classmates, with those who have both taught and learned from you, and also with the community beyond the university's walls.

I can already anticipate a future in which you will make your unique and collective contributions in serving and leading this nation.

The word *university* derives from a Latin root that means "whole; entire." Although many think of a university as bricks and mortar and the people who inhabit them, we capture something more profound if we include the entire community in our scope.

From this perspective, our responsibility *to share* our learning comes into sharper focus. That responsibility arises from the simple fact that not everyone in our society has the same opportunities.

The world is changing at a breathtaking pace. As we speed into the 21st century, our lives are increasingly permeated by sophisticated and complex technologies. They have changed our institutions and made our world smaller. The level of knowledge and skills needed to flourish is growing at an accelerating rate, making lifelong learning an exciting fact of life.

To cope with these challenges and ensure our common prosperity, we will need the talents of *everyone*. We can't afford to leave a single person behind. In particular, we need to foster the strength that diversity brings to our national purpose. Diversity is our nation's competitive advantage, and we must capitalize on it. Crossing societal and disciplinary boundaries is where the action lies.

All of us desire to do something with our lives that makes a difference. One thing *all of us* can do is to mentor someone else. Mentoring is giving back. Mentoring matters to the individuals we guide and the society that will benefit. That's as good as it gets!

In this sense, you are not leaving the university at all. You remain within it and yet enlarge it throughout your lives.

Today, knowledge is both the source of inspiration and the object of aspirations worldwide. People everywhere in the world see the capacity to create, integrate, and use knowledge as their best chance to foster economic prosperity and improve the quality of life. We know that new knowledge is a key force driving innovation. In fact, Peter Drucker defines innovation as applying new knowledge to things that are new and different.

The economist Joseph Schumpeter, writing in the 1930s, coined the phrase "creative destruction" to describe the process by which innovation disrupts—and displaces—old technologies and practices as new ones emerge. The old gives way to the new as a necessary feature of economic growth.

But innovation is not an abstract force. It's what *people* do. So we can speak instead of *creative transformation*. That's what drives change. When the best in human nature is the vital spirit shaping progress, innovation is at its best.

When you're innovating, keep this thought in mind: Having the skill to do things right *is not enough;* doing the right thing *must be your aim.*

There's a lesson here. If you don't transform the world yourself, someone else will. If you want the world to reflect your vision and your ideals, you will have to roll up your sleeves and become an innovator. But when you're innovating, keep this thought in mind: Having the skill *to do things right* is not enough; *doing the right thing* must be your aim.

A surprising and wonderful feature of innovation is that each one of you can *do it*—not in fifteen years, not in ten years—but *tomorrow*.

The bit of wisdom I want to leave with you today is how to do this. It's really quite straightforward: *Challenge the world you're given.*

Probe the accepted way of doing things, while appreciating the opportunity to effect change given to you by those who preceeded you. (In other words, give some respect to your elders as you poke the frontier.) Innovation takes agility, tenacity, and a deft touch. Muhammad Ali's famous words of advice apply here: "Float like a butterfly, sting like a bee"—the butterfly beautiful and the sting sweet.

In science and engineering, we do this by testing boundaries and exploring new frontiers to advance knowledge. The most successful businesses compete in much the same way. In human affairs, we depend on the to-and-fro of dialogue and the free exchange of ideas to keep our society vital and on-track. And in the arts, we see innovation taken to its most expressive edge.

The vision of innovation is not limited to molecules and machines. We need innovation in our schools—in new ways to mentor and new tools for learning. We need innovation in industry—in cleaner and more efficient processes and products. We need innovation in the humanities, in the arts, in business, and in our public and private institutions. It's the lifeblood of our civilization.

At UMBC, you've been respected for your curiosity and imagination, and you've been encouraged to think both independently and interdependently. That's the best preparation you could have to be an innovator.

One of our great American essayists, Ralph Waldo Emerson, put it this way: "Do not go where the path may lead, go instead where there is no path and leave a trail."

Of course, there are risks in challenging the status quo. In our efforts to plough new ground, we sometimes make mistakes. In those moments of failure, we may doubt ourselves.

The sometimes gloomy, but ever thoughtful cartoon character Charlie Brown expresses these moments perfectly when he says, "Sometimes I lie awake at night, and I ask, 'Where have I gone wrong?' Then a voice says to me, 'This is going to take more than one night.'"

I suspect all of us have experienced these "dark moments of the soul." One look at the news will remind us that not all change is for the better. Our troubled times, marked by the tragedy of 9/11, tell us plainly and clearly that not all is right with humankind.

But soul-felt innovation can lift our spirits and show us a way through. There are always unknown territories to explore and as yet unimagined paths to a common good. When we question and challenge old ways in order to imagine and create new ones, we can move the whole world in a direction that makes it better.

So, don't ever be afraid of swimming against the current. You may discover that it's not just the world you transform in the process, but yourselves as well.

Let me celebrate the Class of 2002 once again with these final words. I congratulate you on a job well done. I wish you a future that is challenging and rewarding, a future that provides you every opportunity to create the life—and the world—you imagine, a future that lets your spirits soar. Best wishes to you all.

Centennial of Flight Kick-Off Event[2]

Marion C. Blakey

Administrator, Federal Aviation Administration, 2002– ; born Gadsden, AL; bachelor's degree with honors in international studies, Mary Washington College of the University of Virginia; attended Johns Hopkins University, School of Advanced International Studies for graduate work in Middle East Affairs; Department of Commerce; Department of Education; National Endowment for the Humanities; White House staff; administrator, Department of Transportation's National Highway Traffic Safety Administration, 1992–93; principal, Blakey & Associates, a public affairs consulting firm focusing on transportation issues and traffic safety, 1993–2001; Chairman, National Transportation Safety Board, 2001–02.

Editors' introduction: December 17, 2003, marks the 100th anniversary of the Wright brothers' first successful flight, and Administrator Blakey helped launch a year-long period of recognition at the National Air and Space Museum in Washington, D.C. After Ms. Blakey "celebrate[d] the qualities of human spirit that made the first flight," she introduced "pioneers of flight" who were in attendance and others who represented them, among them Don Lopez, former fighter pilot and deputy director of the National Air and Space Museum; Colonel Charles McGee, representing the Tuskegee Airmen; astronaut John Glenn; and astronaut and U.S. Air Force Colonel Pamela Melroy.

Marion C. Blakey's speech: Today, we begin a celebration that marks a century of extraordinary accomplishment in powered flight. As we celebrate a century of achievement, all of us at the FAA are working to chart the next century of flight . . . with improved safety . . . more capacity . . . and greater efficiency than ever before. This is the mission of the nearly 50,000 dedicated professionals across the FAA workforce—and they make it all possible.

But, today, we celebrate the qualities of human spirit that made the first flight, and the billions of flights following, a reality. We celebrate the pioneers, visionaries, and adventurers that dreamed about the possibility and created reality.

---

2. Delivered on December 17, 2002, at Washington, D.C.

For the next year we will honor the accomplishments of the many men and women who were—and still are—key members of the aviation community. From dreamer to scientist, from aviator to astronaut, we will share these inspirational stories of accomplishment with the world.

Here to represent the qualities of the human spirit they embody is a group of special people, whom we asked to join us today; they symbolize the countless men and women who have brought us this far . . . and promise to take us so much farther.

To help us recognize these aviation pioneers and the men and women they represent, I would like to ask another American hero, Don Lopez, former fighter pilot and ace and current Deputy Director of the National Air and Space Museum, to join me along with the fifth grade honor students from Parkview and Sligo Elementary Schools in Washington, D.C.

> *It was Charles Lindbergh who proved to the world that in a world of daring, anything is possible.*

Charles Lindbergh once asked, "What kind of man would live where there is no daring?" And, it was Charles Lindbergh who proved to the world that in a world of daring, anything is possible. He and many other pilots faced extreme risk as they opened our eyes to the opportunities of aviation. Lindbergh proved that we could bridge the ocean, and thus the world.

Representing the many courageous men and women who set out to prove to the world that there is no such word as *impossible* is aviation's "Lone Eagle," Charles Lindbergh, represented today by his grandson, Erik Lindbergh.

The events of 1903 marked the beginning of a new age of transportation for the world. It was in the 1920s that Henry Ford helped bring aviation to the public by developing early passenger transport aircraft, such as the Ford Tri-motor. Along with compatriots, like Glenn Curtiss and William Boeing, Henry Ford pioneered the successful adaptation of the basic concept of the airplane. He brought aviation and its benefits within the reach of the average citizen.

Representing those early thought leaders who saw flight as a viable means of transportation and were key to its success, is Ford Motor Company founder Henry Ford, represented today by his great grandson Edsel B. Ford the Second.

From the day Amelia Earhart became impassioned with flight she sought to prove that the sky was not the limit . . . but the beginning. Her accomplishments not only opened the eyes of the world to the possibilities of flight, but to the capabilities of women as well. For her and other early flight pioneers, it took a strong sense of adventure and determination to accept risk in the face of uncertainty.

Representing those who realize the beauty and sense of adventure that flight offers, and choose to share it with the world, is aviation pioneer Amelia Earhart, represented today by her niece Amy Kleppner.

The Ninety-Nines is an organization founded in 1929 by 99 licensed women pilots for the mutual support and advancement of aviation. Amelia Earhart was a founder and the first president. Today, eight of the founders are still living. All members are dedicated to promoting world fellowship through flight, providing opportunities for women, and preserving the unique history of women in aviation.

Representing the spirit of camaraderie and the immense joy that flight can bring—as well as the heritage of women in aviation—is the president of the Ninety-Nines, Jody McCarrell.

The Tuskegee Airmen volunteered to become America's first African-American military airmen. During World War II, they never lost a bomber they escorted into battle—a feat unmatched in their time.

In accepting the challenge, each one displayed skill and determination while enduring the doubt and prejudice of many of their fellow soldiers. Their drive to earn the respect of their critics, much like the Wright brothers, was an early force in creating historic social change within the armed forces and throughout America.

Representing the Tuskegee Airmen for their determination to fight for freedom is Colonel Charles McGee, member of the 302d fighter squadron.

On February 20th, 1962, the world waited in anticipation as a human orbited the earth for the first time, extending our freedoms into uncharted territory. Thirty-six years later, John Glenn proved that such freedom was not bound by age. Astronaut Glenn had also been a distinguished pilot in the Marine Corps, fighting for the inherent right of freedom for all mankind. The efforts of astronauts and military pilots have and will continue to extend the reaches of freedom for the entire world.

Representing the thousands of pilots around the world who seek to provide freedom in all of its forms is Senator John Glenn.

Thousands of hours of research, experimentation, and trial led to the eventual success of the Wright brothers' first flight. Like those before and after them, the Wright brothers knew that achieving their dream would require hard work and a commitment to the scientific process. For almost 100 years, we have capitalized on the benefits of flight to seek a better understanding of the world around us. And, for almost 100 years we have counted on the persistence of researchers and scientists to provide the knowledge necessary for us to do so.

Representing researchers and scientists who view knowledge as the most successful road to advancement is NASA chief scientist Dr. Shannon Lucid.

Winston Churchill once said, "Courage is rightly esteemed the first of human qualities, because it is the quality which guarantees all others." Indeed, the accomplishment of flight, to serve and protect, has come only from great courage shown by people willing to push aviation to its extreme. Brigadier General David Lee "Tex"

Hill, who stands among America's top fighter aces, represents the astonishing bravery that, to fighter pilots, simply "goes with the territory."

Without question, flight is represented by countless heroes who have stirred greatness in others.

As a member of the renowned Flying Tigers, and more broadly our armed services, General Hill represents the courage that has guaranteed enduring liberty in our nation.

Representing the courageous men and women who serve as pilots in the armed forces is Brigadier General David Lee "Tex" Hill.

The quest to discover uncharted territory drives innovation. Like the countless pioneers before them, our pioneers of space exploration set foot on lands that had never before been touched by humans. From our first entry into outer space and our presence on the moon, to our future efforts to set foot on Mars and beyond, the spirit of discovery propels the hearts of astronauts to take those strides for all of us.

Representing those pioneers of air and space who strive to discover new worlds is Dr. Neil Armstrong.

From the inception of the Wright Brothers Aeroplane Company in 1909, to the institution of NASA, the aerospace industry provides us with remarkable moments of innovation and products of invention.

The vision of the aerospace industry reaches far and wide, providing expertise in everything from research to defense and exploration to efficiency. It is a business full of heroes unknown to the common citizen, but one that deserves tremendous recognition for its contributions to modern society.

Representing those organizations that create a vision for our future in air and space is Dr. Vance Coffman, CEO and chairman of Lockheed Martin Corporation.

It has been said that a hero is best defined as a person noted for feats of courage or nobility of purpose, especially one who has risked or sacrificed his or her life. And while the act of courage takes on many forms, it is the hero who stands as an example and inspiration for our youth as they mature into active members of society. Without question, flight is represented by countless heroes who have stirred greatness in others.

Representing those pioneers of flight whose driving force includes a strong desire to inspire our youth is NASA astronaut and U.S. Air Force Colonel Pamela Melroy.

It was a dream that had been waiting to be realized for thousands of years, and chased by countless visionaries, scholars, and brave souls. But even as the mass of collected knowledge came to a crucial turning point, it was not until the ingenuity of the Wright brothers that the puzzle of powered flight was solved.

Discovery requires deep understanding, constant interpretation of knowledge, and unbridled persistence. And, it's when these qualities come together that defining moments—true achievements—occur. The Wright brothers are among a league of heroes that inspired the world to follow their dreams with passion, courage, and resolve.

Representing those unique individuals whose achievements are born from dreams and inspired by a quest for freedom are Orville and Wilbur Wright, represented today by their great grand-niece, Amanda Wright Lane.

Ladies and gentlemen, please join me in applauding these pioneers of flight and the countless people they represent.

Tribute to the Astronauts of the Space Shuttle *Columbia*[3]

Chris Dodd

U.S. senator from Connecticut, 1980– ; born Willimantic, CT, May 27, 1944; B.A. in English Literature, Providence College, 1966; J.D., University of Louisville School of Law, 1972; member, Peace Corps, Dominican Republic, 1966–68; U.S. Army reserves, 1969–75; practiced law in New London, CT, 1973–74; member, U.S. Congress, 1975–80; member of Senate committees: Foreign Relations; Rules and Administration; Health, Education, Labor, and Pensions; Banking, Housing, and Urban Affairs; Securities and Investment subcommittee; Foreign Relations subcommittee on Western Hemisphere, Peace Corps, and Narcotics; Senate Children's Caucus; chairman, Democratic National Committee; member, Whitewater commission; Edmund S. Muskie Distinguished Public Service Award; Hubert H. Humphrey Public Service Award.

Editors' introduction: On January 16, 2003, Space Shuttle *Columbia* mission STS-107 was launched for a 16-day journey dedicated to research in physical life and space sciences. Aboard *Columbia* were six Americans and Israel's first astronaut, Ilan Ramon. On the morning of February 1, during its return to Earth, NASA Administrator Sean O'Keefe reported "a loss of communications at a little after 9:00 A.M." *Columbia* had broken up in flames over Texas, killing the seven crew members and spreading debris over three states. Senator Dodd reflected on the tragedy while speaking on the floor of the U.S. Senate. After outlining successes and failures experienced in the past, Senator Dodd counseled that "the space program must go on," and that the seven *Columbia* astronauts "gave their lives that humanity could take yet another leap forward into the vast unknown of future knowledge."

Chris Dodd's speech: Mr. President, I rise today to join the nation in grieving the tragic loss of the crew of the space shuttle *Columbia*, which went down during its return to Earth after 16 days in space.

My heart especially goes out to the families of the seven astronauts on board the *Columbia*—Rick Husband, the mission commander, William McCool, the shuttle pilot, and the five crew members, David Brown, Michael Anderson, Laurel Clark, Kalpana Chawla, and Ilan Ramon.

---

3. Delivered on February 4, 2003, at Washington, D.C.

Mr. President, ever since President Kennedy announced, on May 25, 1961, that the United States would land an American safely on the Moon by the end of the 1960s, our nation has been committed to reaching for the stars.

President Kennedy said, "We choose to go to the Moon . . . not because [it is] easy, but because [it is] hard."

Thus began America's space program, a program which has compelled some of our nation's brightest and bravest souls to risk their lives in the name of progress; to travel into the frontiers of space in order to advance human life here on Earth.

The space program has seen its share of tragedy. In the pre–space travel days of the 1950s, daredevil pilots, such as former Senator John Glenn, risked it all to help us develop jet engine and rocket propulsion technologies, and to learn about the outer reaches of our stratosphere. Dozens died in the process. They sacrificed their lives to make the space program possible.

Many of us are old enough to remember January 27, 1967—the day *Apollo 1* exploded during a launch-pad test, killing all three astronauts on board, Virgil Grissom, Edward White, and Roger Chaffee. I personally remember the numbness I felt when hearing the news, and later watching the tragedy replayed on television.

But the space program went forward. Eighteen months later, on July 20, 1969, Neil Armstrong and Buzz Aldrin took man's first steps on the Moon.

All of a sudden, our boundaries seemed limitless.

In 1982, the space shuttle program became operational, and trips to space began seeming commonplace.

But once again, on January 28, 1986, our nation mourned the loss of shuttle astronauts Michael Smith, Dick Scobee, Judith Resnik, Ronald McNair, Ellison Onizuka, Gregory Jarvis, and Christa McAuliffe, who were lost when the *Challenger* shuttle exploded during take-off.

President Reagan's words spoke for an entire nation when he said: "We've grown used to the idea of space, and perhaps we forget that we've only just begun. We are still pioneers."

With those words, the space shuttle program went forward, and there have been dozens of shuttle launches over the past 15 years, reaping untold rewards for humanity in terms of increasing our understanding of physics, biology, and of the physical universe in which we live.

Now we are in the shadow of another tragedy. Some are questioning whether or not manned space flights ought to continue. Some say the risks to the lives of the astronauts outweigh the gains we can make in terms of scientific progress.

I say we listen to the families of those lost on space shuttle *Columbia*. They are united in their feelings that their loved ones died doing what they loved most—that these heroes understood the risks, but were undeterred because they also understood the potential for gain.

These families are united in their belief that the space program must go on.

I believe that if it does not, than the lives of these seven astronauts would have been lost in vain.

Tragedies like these are a direct result of America's restless desire for progress—to go further, fly faster, learn more, and advance.

Robert Kennedy once said: "It is from acts of courage that human history is shaped."

These seven brave astronauts knew the risks. They were not deterred. They were emboldened. They gave their lives that humanity could take yet another leap forward into the vast unknown of future knowledge.

They are, and always will be, national heroes.

Mr. President, I would like to submit for the record seven articles from Sunday's *New York Times*, each of which offers insights into the lives and personal accomplishments of each of the astronauts lost in Saturday's tragedy.

> *Tragedies like these are a direct result of America's restless desire for progress—to go further, fly faster, learn more, and advance.*

Reading through them, I couldn't help but be struck by the diversity of the crew. Once upon a time, all NASA astronauts were white men from the military. But over the past few decades, NASA has been recruiting astronauts based on their skills, their excellence, and of course, their courage and commitment. That has meant a more diverse astronaut pool.

The crew of the *Columbia* were a wonderful example of this diversity—men and women, black and white, immigrant and native-born, as well as a crew member from Israel, Ilan Ramon.

The crew of the *Columbia* offer us a reminder that there are no boundaries in space, and that humans are one race.

Together, we will overcome this tragedy. And together, we will continue to look toward the stars and beyond.

The Astronauts

Colonel Rick Husband, the commander of the *Columbia* mission, bravely served our country as a colonel in the air force prior to joining NASA. After trying four times to become an astronaut, he was finally successful in 1994, and flew his first space mission on the shuttle *Discovery* in 1999. Rick was a dedicated astronaut who studied for his mission at all times, even during Christmas. However, he was also a dedicated family man who leaves behind his wife, Evelyn, and two children.

Navy Commander William McCool was the pilot of the *Columbia*. William graduated second in his class at the Naval Academy and was a seasoned test pilot. In 1996, he joined NASA's astronaut program and trained for several years before finally receiving his first chance to pilot a space shuttle. William was a dedicated member of the *Columbia* crew who was fond of athletics and chess, and he will be sorely missed by his wife, three children, and by all Americans.

Captain David Brown was also a navy doctor, and joined the astronaut program in 1996. David was multi-talented, and an example of success in all his endeavors. During college, he earned top marks in biology and was also a member of the circus—performing as an acrobat, unicyclist, and stilt walker. Although navy doctors are rarely selected for pilot training, he graduated first in his naval aviation class, and flew a number of navy planes throughout his career. On the *Columbia*, David was a key member of the scientific research team. His zest for life and talent for science will be sorely missed, but not forgotten.

Dr. Laurel Salton Clark was a navy officer who had an impressive career that included diving with the Navy SEALs, conducting medical evacuations from submarines, and taking on the role of a flight surgeon. She was one of two women on board the *Columbia* and took part in a variety of life-science experiments aboard the shuttle. Laurel is survived by her husband, Jonathan, and a son. However, this amazing woman, who was nicknamed "floral" for her propensity to wear vibrant colors, will never be forgotten.

Dr. Kalpana Chawla was an American who was born in India. From a young age, she dreamed of becoming an astronaut. Kalpana moved to the United States to attend college, and during this time, she received her doctorate in aerospace engineering from the University of Colorado and became an American citizen. She joined NASA in 1994, and was the first Indian-born woman in space. While on the *Columbia*, she was responsible for operating the robotic arm of the shuttle and was an invaluable member of the shuttle team. Although an American citizen, Dr. Chawla was also a national hero in India and will remain dear to all of our hearts.

Lt. Colonel Michael Anderson was another example of the diversity of the American space program. An African American who grew up in a predominantly white city, Michael received his master's degree in physics from Creighton University in 1990. He dreamed of becoming an astronaut from the age of three and took the first step towards fulfillment of his dream in 1994, when he joined NASA's shuttle program. Michael had previously been on a shuttle mission, and in 1998, he helped the crew of the *Endeavour* transfer equipment to the *Mir* Space Station. Although he leaves behind his wife, Sandra, Michael's success will continue to serve as an inspiration to all Americans.

Colonel Ilan Ramon was an example of the strong bond and cooperation between America and one of its staunchest allies, Israel. A former Israeli Air Force pilot, Ilan was the son and grandson of Holocaust survivors, and the first Israeli in space. He was selected as an astronaut candidate in 1997 and spent more than four years living in America while preparing for this mission. Although his death is a tragic loss to his wife, Rona, his four children, and the nation of Israel, he will forever be remembered as a hero to his people and a representation of the strong bonds between our two countries.

Commemorating the *Columbia* Astronauts[4]

Kay Bailey Hutchison

U.S. senator from Texas, 1993– ; born Galveston, TX, July 22, 1943; B.A., University of Texas, 1962; LLB, University of Texas Law School, 1967; TV news reporter, Houston, TX, 1969–71; private law practice, 1969–74; Texas House of Representatives, 1972–76; Texas state treasurer, 1990; vice chairman, Senate Republican Conference, 2001; U.S. delegate, Helsinki Commission on Security and Cooperation in Europe; Senate committees include Veterans' Affairs; chair, Military Construction subcommittee; defense subcommittee of Senate Appropriations; subcommittee on Aviation and Commerce; chair, Surface Transportation and Merchant Marine subcommittee; authored opinion pieces on tax policy, transportation, foreign policy, and national security issues in New York Times, Wall Street Journal, Washington Post, Los Angeles Times, *and London's* Financial Times; *Republican Woman of the Year, 1995; Texas Women's Hall of Fame, 1997; Advocate for Education Award from the College Board, 1999; National Military Family Association Award for Service to Military Families, 2001; Woodrow Wilson Award for Public Service, 2003.*

Editors' introduction: Returning from space on February 1, 2003, about 207,135 feet from Earth, space shuttle *Columbia* disintegrated over Texas, killing its seven crew members. In the weeks to come, investigators would ask what led to the failure of the shuttle, including questioning reductions in funding for the space program. But four days after the tragic loss, in a speech on the Senate floor Senator Hutchison "honor[ed] the memory and the sacrifice of the seven astronauts." She stated, "The American spirit knows no bounds. . . . We will continue to explore the vast sky that envelops the earth, and their names will forever be etched into the history of space flight."

Kay Bailey Hutchison's speech: Mr. President, today I rise to honor the memory and the sacrifice of the seven astronauts whose lives were tragically cut short in pursuit of the newest frontier—space.

---

4. Delivered on February 5, 2003, at Washington, D.C.

America is a word, a country, and a people. America is also a spirit, an indomitable spirit of adventure and courage, one that defies complacency and accepts challenge. The American spirit knows no bounds.

Israeli astronaut Ilan Ramon also had that spirit, and so did Kalpana Chawla, who was born in India and made America her home. It is that spirit which President Kennedy harnessed in 1961 when he made the bold claim: Within a decade, America would put a man on the Moon and return him safely home.

On Saturday, we were reminded of the high price we sometimes pay for reaching new horizons.

That same spirit enabled us to fulfill a great mission and make space travel seem routine, although it was never routine.

It is that spirit which fueled the hearts and minds of those seven men and women who launched into the sky on January 6 [sic], 2003.

On Saturday, we were reminded of the high price we sometimes pay for reaching new horizons. Our thirst for knowledge led us to explore space. Our curiosity, sense of wonderment, and desire to improve life on Earth prompted us time and again to defy the odds. Those heroes did not take their task lightly, but they undertook it with joy.

Ilan Ramon, the first Israeli astronaut, who was on that fated flight, wrote the following words from space:

"The world looks marvelous from up here, so peaceful, so wonderful and so fragile."

His serene vision came to a catastrophic end on Saturday morning, and that moment when the world awoke to the news that seven astronauts disappeared into the skies will be one etched in our collective memories forever.

In recent years, America has borne too much tragedy and experienced too much grief, but our collective loss still sears our souls and the pain is never easier to bear. Today, just 4 short days after they vanished into the crystal blue skies of Texas, we pause to remember them and thank them from our hearts: Rick Husband, Kalpana Chawla, Laurel Clark, Ilan Ramon, William McCool, David Brown, and Michael Anderson.

And though the families' loss cannot be diminished, their pain and grief is shared around the world, and our prayers are with them.

Their sacrifice will never be forgotten. Their lives were not lost in vain. We will send more brave astronauts into the cosmos to learn and discover. We will continue to explore the vast sky that envelops the earth, and their names will forever be etched into the history of space flight.

Rick Husband, a spiritual man, a Texan, the commander of the space shuttle *Columbia*, often signed photos referencing Proverbs 3:5-6: "Trust in the Lord with all your heart and lean not on your own understanding; acknowledge Him in all your ways and He will direct your paths."

Throughout history, our young nation has experienced great heartache and tragedy. Each time, we have overcome adversity with boldness and tenacity. We have come back stronger than ever.

With steely resolve and a firm determination, we rose from the ashes and embers of Ground Zero more resolute than ever before.

Christina Rossetti, the 18th-century poet, wrote a poem called "Remember." She could never have envisioned what this poem would come to represent, but it did bring me some solace in this time of tragedy in my home state of Texas. She wrote:

> Remember me when I am gone away,
> Gone far away into the silent land;
> When you can no more hold me by the hand,
> Nor I half turn to go yet turning stay.
> Remember me when no more day by day
> You tell me of our future that you planned;
> Only remember me; you understand
> It will be late to counsel then or pray.
> Yet if you should forget me for a while
> And afterwards remember, do not grieve:
> For if the darkness and corruption leave
> A vestige of the thoughts that I once had,
> Better by far you should forget and smile
> Than that you should remember and be sad.

We will hold these seven souls in our hearts and eventually we will smile again. We will rise from the ashes in the fields of Texas, Louisiana, and Arkansas. The quest for space exploration will not end with this tragedy. It will live on, it will prosper, for it is our duty, our calling, and our destiny.

Yesterday, like so many members of the Senate and House, along with the president of the United States and our first lady, I attended a beautiful ceremony where we saw firsthand the families and the realization of their personal loss. We were uplifted by seeing the greatness of what these astronauts had done and what they are doing for the future of our country and our world. It is much bigger than just those seven astronauts, which I think their families and they themselves believed. They know this was a higher calling and that their sacrifices will lay the groundwork for a better space shuttle, a better space station, America staying preeminent in the world in national security and in medical research. I think they knew they were contributing to the future of our country.

The ceremony yesterday really began our time of closure, our time to pay the respects to those brave young men and women who were willing to make this sacrifice for their children and their future generations, and to say that America is going to renew our commitment. America is going to stay in the forefront, because we know if a country is static it will begin to fall behind. We know we have been the first to reap so many benefits from space exploration, which we have shared with the world. We know there are many more innovations to come and that America will be there to find those discoveries.

Confronting Uncertainty[5]

Richard C. Levin

President (1993–) and Frederick William Beinecke professor of economics, Yale University, 1992– ; born San Francisco, CA, April 7, 1947; B.A. in history, Stanford University, 1968; bachelor of letters in politics and philosophy, Oxford University, 1971; Ph.D. in economics, Yale University, 1974; teaching, research, and administration on the Yale University faculty, 1974– ; research associate, National Bureau of Economic Research, Cambridge, MA, 1985–90; chairman, Economics Department, Yale University, 1987–92; program director, International Institute of Applied Systems Analysis, Vienna, 1990–92; dean, Graduate School of Arts and Sciences, Yale University, 1992–93; fellow of the American Academy of Arts and Sciences, and member of its Board of Science, Technology, and Economic Policy; trustee, William and Flora Hewlett Foundation; Blue Ribbon Panel on the Economics of Baseball; has written on intellectual property rights, the patent system, industrial research and development, and the effects of antitrust and public regulation on private industry.

Editors' introduction: On September 11, 2001, thousands of people were killed by terrorist assaults on New York City, Washington, D.C., and Shanksville, Pennsylvania. In response, President Bush first sent troops into Afghanistan, and then to Iraq. While a majority of American citizens apparently supported the administration's policy in Iraq, many individuals and organizations, particularly on college campuses, opposed the war. Nearly two months after the conflict with Iraq had officially ended, in his Baccalaureate Address at Yale University, President Levin reminded the graduating seniors they had "entered Yale at a time of great optimism, and you leave at a time of great uncertainty." He nevertheless expressed confidence that "You are now prepared to move beyond your Yale adventure to challenges that were unforseen four years ago, as we heralded the revolutions in science and technology that continue to hold out so much hope for the future."

Richard C. Levin's speech: Four years ago, when I welcomed you at your Freshman Assembly, I reflected the widespread optimism that accompanied our entry into a new millennium. I spoke of the potential of the Information Revolution to raise the standard of liv-

5. Delivered on May 24–25, 2003, in Woolsey Hall at New Haven, CT. Reprinted with permission of Yale University.

ing here and around the world, and I heralded the coming Genetics Revolution and its potential for dramatic improvement in human health. I suggested that the economic and social impact of these developments would equal or exceed that of the Industrial Revolution of the 18th century, the building of the railroads in the 19th century, and the invention and diffusion of the automobile in the 20th century.

I would still stand by this prediction, but how very different the world seems four years later. The challenges we have all faced, both outside and within the university, were not those we expected four years ago. Shortly after you came to Yale, our rapidly growing economy sputtered to a halt. Unemployment increased, and the stock markets tumbled. Then came the appalling attacks on the World Trade Center and the Pentagon, the anthrax scare, military intervention in Afghanistan, and the war in Iraq. Meanwhile, the campus was saddened this January by the tragic death of four students in an auto accident and shocked this week by a bombing at the Law School.

The challenges we have all faced, both outside and within the university, were not those we expected four years ago.

You entered Yale at a time of great optimism, and you leave at a time of great uncertainty. The opportunities presented by the revolutions in information technology and genetics persist, and they will be yours to make the most of in the years ahead. But these opportunities will be most productively pursued in an environment of reduced uncertainty, and the creation of such an environment will require clarity, wisdom, and ingenuity.

Despite America's unprecedented military power, the principles defining the geopolitical order of the planet remain uncertain—in part because of America's ambivalence about its role in the world and in part because of the world's ambivalence about America's power. Is the future to be guided by a unilateralist America, or by a wider community of nations? Is America's objective to spread democratic institutions throughout the world, or is it merely to unseat the most egregious of tyrants? Can peace in the Middle East be achieved, and, if it is, will terrorism subside? Finding the answers to these questions will require our best efforts—your best efforts.

When I greeted you four years ago, I related the story of Edward Whymper, the 19th-century British mountaineer who, at the age of 25 after seven unsuccessful attempts, made the first ascent of the Matterhorn. I provided you with examples of Whymper's curiosity, resourcefulness, and analytic thinking to inspire you to prepare for the challenges of revolutionary time. But in fact the lessons derived from Whymper's experience are no less relevant to the challenging uncertainties we confront today. Let me reinforce these lessons by recalling what I told you once before:

"Perhaps the most impressive demonstration of Whymper's curiosity, resourcefulness, and analytic thinking is his discussion of how, after seven failed attempts to climb the Matterhorn from the southwest, he decided to attack the mountain from the northeast. From this direction, the perspective represented in most photographs, the mountain appears to be utterly inaccessible, yet it yielded to Whymper's first attempt. What led him to take a new approach? First, he noticed that snow accumulated on the steep eastern face of the mountain, despite what appeared to be a slope of 60 to 70 degrees. By hiking to untraveled passes both north and south of the mountain, he confirmed that the slope, despite appearances, was no more than 40 degrees. Second, he observed that the strata of rock in the mountain were not parallel to the ground; instead, they sloped upward from southwest to northeast. This meant that the ledges, and the possible hand and footholds that they offered, sloped inward on the northeast side, making them easier for the climber than on the more frequently attempted route.

"In this example there are many lessons that bear on your [life's] adventure. You can turn repeated failure into success if you are curious enough, resourceful enough, and analytic enough to look at things in a new way. You have to think outside the box. Don't take received opinion for granted. Look at problems from all perspectives, and use the power of reason to draw inferences. Ask questions, and don't hesitate to accept surprising answers if your observations have been careful and your reasoning has been rigorous."

I have every confidence that you have lived by these lessons these past four years. Curiosity is in abundant supply here. In your course work, at masters' teas and public lectures, and in conversations with your classmates, every one of you has encountered new ideas and new perspectives. And your decisions to embrace, reject, or modify them have shaped your lives. Your resourcefulness is manifest everywhere, in the dozens of new student organizations created by members of your class. Two of you mobilized 66 Yale undergraduates to devote 18,000 hours to tutoring Fair Haven fifth graders in mathematics; another member of your class established a health education program in four local high schools. And as for developing the capacity for analytic thinking—this is nothing less than the primary purpose of the whole curriculum.

Let me take a moment to remind you of the special attributes of the place that has given you ample room to exercise and develop these qualities of open-mindedness, initiative, and critical thinking. Yale, like other great American universities, is a laboratory for free expression, a microcosm of the values we proclaim as the greatest treasures of our constitutional democracy. When the Iraqi war began, I wrote the following words to the entire Yale community:

"In an environment of civility, where we respect and listen carefully to one another, controversy stimulates learning. We need to leave ample space for free expression and bring the tools of reason and analysis to bear on the arguments we hear. In the weeks to come, let us, as a university community, continue to model the free, open, and tolerant society that the United States at its best represents. And let us also learn from this experience of war, through reflection and conversation."

I'm proud of the way we modeled freedom, openness, and toleration during the past two months. Although there were a small number of incidents in which students were harassed because of their political views, the prevailing atmosphere was one of civility, respect, and a desire to learn. Thanks to the efforts of John Gaddis and Cynthia Farrar and many others, we held 12 teach-ins concerned with various aspects of the war, Iraqi civilization, global governance, nation-building, and patriotism. These provided the community an opportunity for learning at a depth not found in the public news media. These lectures and panel discussions are still worthy of your attention, and all are available in video on the Yale Web site.

The environment we create within the American university is a powerful instrument for mutual understanding among nations.

The environment we create within the American university is a powerful instrument for mutual understanding among nations. We have nearly 1,800 international students at Yale, and a comparable number of visiting scholars. For many of them, Yale is the first place they have ever lived where they can truly speak their minds, where they can challenge the authority of teachers, where ideas alone prevail—not status, rank, power, or privilege. This struck me forcefully in my conversations last fall with the first cohort of Yale World Fellows. This group of emerging leaders included former cabinet ministers from Peru and Ecuador, the founder of a micro-lending bank in India, a television anchorperson from Cameroon, and a law school dean from China. By their own testimony, the first group of fellows returns home with a deep appreciation of the values of a democratic society; many of them reported experiencing genuinely free expression and freedom of inquiry for the first time.

In the wake of September 11, our government has understandably required more careful scrutiny of those seeking to enter the country on student visas. It has also, through the PATRIOT Act and various administrative rulings, begun to restrict the range of subjects that students from certain countries can study and the types of materials they can work with in university laboratories. One recognizes the legitimate concerns for safety and security that drive these changes in policy, but at the same time one worries about excessively restricting who may study here and what they may study.

There will be good reasons for denying entry to some prospective students, but we should remember that an enduring peace requires mutual understanding, and there is no better guarantee of peace than to ensure that the leaders of the next generation have an opportunity to learn from one another during the formative periods of their lives. There is less reason to deny students, once enrolled here, access to the full range of our curriculum and research activities. Unfortunate as it would be to deny visas to promising students who may learn from exposure to a free and open society, it would be even more unfortunate to have such students denied the very freedom we hope they will come to appreciate.

You have had the privilege these past four years of living and working under conditions that gave you almost unlimited opportunity to exercise your curiosity and resourcefulness and to develop your capacity to think critically. You are now prepared to move beyond your Yale adventure to challenges that were unforeseen four years ago, as we heralded the revolutions in science and technology that continue to hold out so much hope for the future. Your task is to shape lives that take full advantage of the liberal education you received here—lives of personal and professional fulfillment, to be sure, but also lives that make a difference in the world. If we are to preserve the freedom that exists in this university and in this nation, if freedom's blessings are to be extended, peacefully, to those who are oppressed, we will need your engagement and your leadership.

Women and men of the Class of 2003: The world is all before you. Your generation has the potential to end hunger, cure disease, and extend the domain of freedom. Yale has prepared you well, but you will need all the intelligence and wisdom you can muster. You can, you must, and you will rise to meet the challenges of these uncertain and revolutionary times.

Cumulative Speaker Index: 2000–2003

A cumulative speaker index to the volumes of *Representative American Speeches* for the years 1937–1938 through 1959–1960 appears in the 1959–1960 volume; for the years 1960–1961 through 1969–1970, see the 1969–1970 volume; for the years 1970–1971 through 1979–1980, see the 1979–1980 volume; for the years 1980–1981 through 1989–1990, see the 1989–1990 volume; and for the years 1990–1991 through 1999–2000, see the 1999–2000 volume.

189

Index